Gathering the Family

Gathering the Family

the

William Holtz

De mortuis nil nisi bonum

University of Missouri Press

Columbia and London

Copyright © 1997 by
The Curators of the University of Missouri
University of Missouri Press, Columbia, Missouri 65201
Printed and bound in the United States of America
All rights reserved
5 4 3 2 1   01 00 99 98 97

Library of Congress Cataloging-in-Publication Data

Holtz, William V.
    Gathering the family / by William Holtz.
        p.   cm.
    ISBN 0-8262-1153-4 (cloth : alk. paper) — ISBN 0-8262-1128-3
(pbk. : alk. paper)
    1. Holtz, William V. — Family. 2. Holtz family. 3. United States
— Social life and customs — 20th century. I. Title.
CT274.H654 H65   1997
929'.2'0973—DC21   97-20025
                                                              CIP

♾™ This paper meets the requirements of the
American National Standard for Permanence of Paper
for Printed Library Materials, Z39.48, 1984.

Designer: Stephanie Foley
Printer and binder: Thomson-Shore, Inc.
Typefaces: Adobe Garamond and Medici Script

IN MEMORIAM

William Cavin Holtz (1910–1957)

No one would have been more surprised . . .

Contents

Acknowledgments

*F*OR SHARING MEMORIES, my sister Sylvia
Mazzaro, my cousins Naomi LaMora and Pat Ollila, and
my uncle Raymond Holtz. For help in translation, Liisa
Erickson. For helping me find time to write, Howard
Hinkel. For borrowings otherwise unacknowledged,
Diana George and Randall Freisinger. For faith that fragments might grow to make a book, Beverly Jarrett. For
assuring me that certain of my pages were intelligible,
Catherine Parke. For helping me search for Chandler,
my daughter Victoria, A. L. Becker, Sue Garner, and
Chandler Matthews. For professional courtesy and gen-
erosity, Robert M. Davis and Robert Erickson. For patient
reading and rereading with me, my wife, Lora. For gathering with me, again and again, my family.

Some essays are reprinted here in slightly altered form
from the following publications: "A Gathering of
Family," *American Scholar;* "Cradle Song, 1939,"
Kenyon Review; "Brother's Keeper," *American Literary
Review;* "Two Fingers," *Missouri Review.*

"If You Were the Only Girl in the World": Words by
Clifford Gray; music by Nat Ayer (1925). "Song not
copyrighted in the United States until 1963; copyright
in dispute August 1983." Bruce Pollock, *Popular Music,
1920–1979,* 3 vols. (Detroit: Gale Research Co., 1985),
1:868.

The quoted lines in the Prologue are from John Berger, "Her Secrets," *The Contemporary Essay*, 3d ed., ed. Donald Hall (Boston: St. Martin's Press, 1995), 46–49. Originally published in *Threepenny Review*.

The photograph of the cabin on p. 24 is by Dan Cullimore.

Some names have been altered in consideration of people still living.

Gathering the Family

Prologue

*I*WOULD MYSELF CALL this little book a family memoir, a history writ small and measured in domestic dimensions. Some librarians, I suspect, will want to catalog it as autobiography, a different kind of little history, one measured in narrowly personal dimensions, which should leave me feeling faintly pretentious, having lived in the main a pretty ordinary academic life. The essays I offer here were written over several years; some were originally freestanding pieces for separate publication; and early on I had wanted to think of my aim as principally biographical as I wrote about these people in my life. These initial efforts now have been marshaled with others that complete the larger intention that I gradually discovered to be latent within all of them. I wandered in to this work by way of a glory-filled summer evening, late in the day and late in the season and, more or less, late in my own life, through which I slipped into a meditation on my grandson, my grandfather, and myself. Next I discovered that I had a story to tell about my grandmother. The rest of the family followed as a matter of course, except that the more I tried to write truly about these others the more I discovered that I must say about myself; and as I became a willing biographer I became perforce a reluctant and intermittent autobiographer. The last piece fell into place just after my

1

mother's death; and in the end I found that all roads had led to the burying ground, that I had written my own personal book of the dead. "Truly," another writer advises me, "we writers are secretaries of death."

"Autobiography," he continues, "begins with a sense of being alone. It is an orphan form." Certainly these essays mark as much a severance as a continuity between me and (the etymology leaps out) my predecessors. Those I have written of are beyond pain or pride in anything I say; and truly I am an orphan now, as most of us are finally, and of an age myself to be beyond most bruises to my own amour propre, even from my own hand. Indeed, the self I must drag upon the page from out of some youthful indiscretions is so long-gone a predecessor that I hardly know him; I summon him as an actor there to testify about his family, not about himself, however much he may want to strut and fret a bit. These were people by most measures as ordinary in their lives as I have been in mine, except that they made an extraordinary impression on me, and I still see them as having been extraordinary in difficult, even heroic ways that I have been largely protected from. Speak only good of the dead, the old Latin maxim admonishes. My intention has been not to idealize these ordinary people but to bear witness to their heroism; though if to bear witness I must speak of myself, and not always to the good, I will accept the liability, and let those who will speak good of me in my turn.

I am conscious of Tolstoy's famous dictum regarding happy and unhappy families. It follows that no writer should find much new to say about the happiness of a family, but much to say about the particular shades of grief and pain he has discovered. In this case, it does follow that I have much to say about my early years and the family I came from, and little about my adult life and the family I have made, which have been more tranquil and rewarding than probably I deserve. It remains to be seen, I suppose, if the common reader finds anything in common with these very particular episodes that I cannot leave alone; but I doubt not that my fellow literary scholars might find material here for lively analyses, along any number of axes, of me and those I write of. I would not preempt these interests, of course, except to say that I have already, I believe, considered many of them on my own, and I blush to imagine that what I have written might be the beneficiary of such great engines of interpretation.

I am willing, however, to share my own most interesting insight, which has been to realize that in the deep background of this enterprise is my childhood reading of the Greek myth of the autochthonous warriors rising from the ground, parentless and fully grown. I am sure that I read this account at just about the time I was also becoming aware, from covert hints and rumors, of the actual nature of my birth, or anyone's. I do recall being much fascinated by the mythic account, imagining myself rising up out of the ground by some vigorous internal power, armed for battle in the world. The alternative account I found pretty scary, in no way allaying the vulnerability of childhood. I will skip over the anthropological implications to say only that for a long time as an adult I found comfort in thinking of myself as, if not autochthonous, certainly autonomous and self-made. I am aware that what I have written here constitutes some kind of reconciliation with the alternative account, embracing my earliest family origins and, ultimately, that fearsome Freudian tale of my father and my mother. Thus, however satisfying the gain in self-knowledge, I have really sought to sink the autobiographical in the biographical as I embed myself in my family past.

Again in my analytical mode as a scholar, I am struck by the relative thinness of the historical material and the richness of memory it has produced, the compulsion by which I have retrieved it. I am reminded, to my embarrassment, of the story of the young writer who, upon meeting Bertrand Russell, confessed that he had been twenty-one before he had known anyone who had written a book: Russell's reply was that *he* had been twenty-one before he had met someone who *hadn't.* I find no distinctive forebears, no extensive lineage, no coherent tradition, no sustaining matrix of relationships, no intention by anyone to leave me anything; yet I have found my memory brimming with more than I could empty upon the page. In those moments when I have thought of my readers, it has been clear that at the forefront have been my own children and grandchildren, for whom I have been trying to discover a usable past in such unpromising materials. Continuity, rather than severance, is the mode; and the orphan autobiographer, delivering his family past into his family present, re-creates himself as biographer and paterfamilias, no longer alone but re-embedded by dint of both parental and filial responsibility in another family this side of the divide. This, then, is a family memoir, written out of my family and into my family; and if the common reader should find it of interest, it may be because (*pace* Tolstoy) not only happy families but all families are in important ways as much alike as not, providing stories not unlike my own. In such a perspective, it must be true that, however unpromising the materials of our lives, we cannot gauge the importance of what we shall leave behind, and in creating a virtual continuity through the absolute disjunctions of death, the writer makes what he must of whatever he has been left.

But to make such a delivery—need I say deliverance?—I have had to make my own past usable, as it is delivered by memory. It was delivered to the care of memory, of course, by people who had little or no intention of making that delivery, while memory, careless of the precisions of history, has now made its re-delivery according to deeply personal imperatives that create its own selective agenda. I understand that memory is neither photographic nor digital, not so much a literal history of experience as a continual dynamic metamorphosis of experience, in which events as precisely datable as newspaper headlines can adhere, in virtual simultaneity, to images vague as a remembered dream. I have had, certainly, other recourse to the fuller amplitude of history: I have kept my own intermittent journals; I have reached for old letters and photos and newspapers; I have sought to verify anecdotes already shaped by prior narrators; but I have had to negotiate—in language, in narrative, subject to all of their imperatives as well—a further reduction and development and redelivery of a version of that palimpsest unrolling in a perpetual present at the back of my mind. Here I find myself at an impasse. My sister has said, on reading some of these pieces, that someday she would like to write her own personal remembrance of the years and the family we shared, which, presumably, would be an account different from mine. Inevitably, however much I try to slip into the background, behind some fixed screen of history, I can only deliver what will hang upon my own primary ur-narrative, already in place, upon which this screen is spread.

Is autobiography then, with all its distortions, inevitable, and despite my evasive efforts to slink to the margins of my account, is this all but a strut and fret before the common reader? Someone has said that no memoirist can write under oath, which must be so if the oath be to history. However, the oath can be only to memory—both what he remembers and how he remembers it. He wants to tell you the way it was the way it is; but he has to tell you his own story, and he has to use his own words.

A Gathering of Family

⁓

*I*T IS THE END OF THE DAY and the end of the summer. We sit, a family gathered, on the screened porch, looking out over the lake. An afternoon storm has just passed; as the evening sky clears in the west the sinking sun catches the clouds still lowering overhead, and suddenly the air about us is bright with gold, a fair shimmering that glows on the lake and the yellowing birches, glistens in the raindrops still caught in the needles of the pines, and even touches our faces with a radiance not our own. We are stricken with the sudden glory; our voices rise and fall in quiet flutterings of delight, like dozing birds roused in our evening tree. Then wonder exhausts our words, and we fall into silence. A moment to remember, I tell myself, as long as I live.

Tomorrow some will leave, and in a few days my wife and I will close the cabin for the winter. But for now, my infant grandson—the first after a series of granddaughters—sits on my lap, looking into my face with the perfect and undiscriminating curiosity that is the privilege of an innocence so lately rocked in fetal waters. His face glows in the golden light. I, no innocent, and long since beached from primal bliss, return his regard with an interest less pure, as I seek in his placid features some resemblance to my own. I am his mother's father, but so far I see mainly signs of his father's family—my daugh-

ter's eyes, perhaps, which, while not my own, seem reminiscent of others in my family. It is an old delusion that passes quickly. What comfort for my decline in some blurred impress of myself on my posterity? Indeed, through the intervening embraces of passion, the liquid exchanges of love, what dilution of my DNA could still work its way in his veins, write my message in his tender flesh? What he finds in my face I cannot guess. The sun settles lower, and I am in shadow.

We have been looking at a book together while the family murmurs in conversation around us. His silken hair and soft cheek have been nestled against my chest as I point to the bright pictures and prompt his talk: *Ooh . . . and what is this big animal?* He looks, and jabs the elephant with a moist finger, and attacks the problem of speech with sounds that will soon be shaped to a language I know. But restless now, he turns his gaze from the book to my face; then, with motives I cannot fathom, he slips off my lap and with spraddled legs and sagging diaper lurches away through the golden light. With a sudden catch at my heart, I find myself brimming with love and vague premonition.

Old bones not my own stir softly inside me. How, I wonder, might my mother's father have asked these questions, and his lineage before him? I have thought sometimes of those movie scenes in which the scion of some great family paces the portrait gallery of his ancestors, where generation upon generation recedes from the brightly lighted present toward some remote but precise origin. But to retrace my line is to halt at the edge of this century, the ocean, and an unknown tongue. Across the gulf of history, geography, and language my people cannot speak to me; and in my mind's eye is no receding gallery but only the brief reaches of childhood memory. In the foreground stands my mother, whose voice I know; in the middle distance my grandfather, whose voice I hear but cannot understand; and at his back only a dark and vacant tunnel of time.

I I

Intermittently for years I have tried to reconstruct him from fragments of memory and casual bits of testimony in family lore. Only twice, do I remember, did he ever even notice me—I was eight that summer—although there must have been other times, earlier, that I cannot recall. But one day that summer I drew near him as he sat in the glassed-in front porch of the little frame house, reading, as he often did, from the big Finnish Bible. I had learned to read and was proud of my skill, but a glance at the page defeated me, as had the alien speech that my mother revived in herself each time we visited. Looking up, he gripped my shoulder with a sudden hand and drew me to him. I remember the furrowed face, dark and suddenly close, the faintly leathery smell of him—it was probably the great leather-bound Bible—and the faded blue eyes looking into mine. Then, with one hand on the page and the other on my shoulder, he began to read to me, a harsh voice rolling over the strange syllables as his finger moved down the page. Uncomfortable, I endured a few moments before I pulled away.

This was in Hancock, Michigan, in 1940. We were there, my mother and I, for most of that summer. Usually, we came for summer visits of a week or so—my father's vacation—from our home in southern Michigan, near the Indiana border, to the little Upper Peninsula copper-mining town that hangs to the hillside above Portage Lake and the ship canal, facing its sister city of Houghton across the water. But this summer we stayed on while my father went home; it was well past the Fourth of July, I know, because I remember hearing from my bed the celebratory dynamite blasts beyond the edge of town: a blasting tradition remained, even though the mines were closed. There had been other visits, too, at least one in the winter, my mother and I, when I was three and my father was out of work, but I have only shards of memory of those times—chiefly of a Christmas tree with actual candles, and of a long, swooping night-time sled ride with my mother down Quincy Hill, past my grandparents' home, and around the corner into Summit Street, where my aunt lived.

My mother was young then, not yet thirty, and she pulled me on the sled up the long Quincy Hill to the top where the old mine buildings still loomed near the road. The cold must have been intense; I can recall it only as a kind of pressure around me, and the long glide down the hill toward the streetlights below was a course through cold tangible in the glittering and shadowy air. My mother tried to get me to walk the few blocks back to my grandparents' house, but I kept sitting down in the snow. Finally she pulled me on the sled, and I was undressed drowsing in front of the warm kitchen range and laid in bed with a hot brick at my feet.

Perhaps the dream came that night. Certainly it came from some time well before my age of continuous memory—a vivid and curious dream, a dream that returned, it seems, often, and that registered itself powerfully not so much in my mind as on my body. I was deep in a cave, far beneath my grandfather's house, and was trying to escape through a tiny opening, a tight tunnel that I tried to wriggle through: I could feel the pressure around my neck and shoulders as I strained to force my way out. . . . Years later, in college, I identified this as a birth-dream, some urgent reconstruction of primal experience in the only terms my imagination could then present to me. By the time I understood it, it had been neutralized, an academic item only, and it did not recur: I sometimes cited it for my students as an instance of unconscious memory. But I can remember, when it did come, waking frightened, lying awake and wondering: what happened next? It seemed that I ought somehow to emerge in my grandfather's basement, where the family was gathered in the summer kitchen, and sit down at the table among them. "Well, here I am," I would say.

III

My grandfather was a dark Finn, short and spare and in his age little more than a scrap of twisted leather topped with a shock of iron-gray hair; as a young man he had been a gymnast, and even in middle age he practiced on homemade parallel bars. His stock was unmixed with the fair and tall Scandinavian type of the other northern countries. Evidence from language tells us that the Finns are Scandinavian only by accident of geography, migration, and recent history: their ancestral home was central Russia—their ancient cousins, by another migration, became the Magyars of modern Hungary—and dark skin and hair and short stature mark these origins in many Finns. Within the culture, *Suomi* is the traditional name for the language and the nation; Tacitus, the first outsider to record notice of them, wrote of a wild and primitive people called *Fenni,* and Finland has been a name imposed on the maps at least since a period of Swedish domination. A later emigration brought many Finns to the United States at the turn of the century—many to escape Russian domination, Finland then being a Russian province, and many to find work in the mines and forests of Michigan, Wisconsin, and Minnesota. Even here they were ethnically distinct, and at the bottom of the immigrant hierarchy; in some lumber camps the Finns were forced to eat at their own tables, the blacks of Scandinavian America, and jokes of their uncleanliness are still current. (How did the Finns come to America? They took a bath, and floated across on the scum.) Doubtless the canard originated in their darker coloring and their determination to stay clean—that is, in their ritual devotion to the sauna, which has become their contribution to American yuppie indulgence.

The sauna was no indulgence for the Finns; rather, it was such a necessity that it was often the first building erected on the tiny farms they cleared. In the towns, neighborhood saunas were quickly established, and makeshift home saunas were cobbled into many basements and garages. The sauna bath was a family occasion like Sunday dinner, and often a social occasion among friends. My uncle had a summer home on the ship canal, that extension of Portage Lake that permits Great Lakes shipping a shortcut through the Keweenaw Peninsula. There was a sauna at the water's edge, and on weekend visits it was my grandfather's privilege to start the fire early in the afternoon and to tend it in the stove improvised from a small metal barrel with rocks on the top. His privilege too to make the bathing switches, not of the traditional birch twigs but of the fragrant tips of white cedar, which grew along that shore. I would see the plume of blue from the chimney, smell the wood smoke rich on the air, while my grandfather moved among the trees, cutting cedar tips with his pocketknife. His privilege, finally, to be the first to enter and bathe: no one could stand the heat he could endure, alone, on the highest bench near the ceiling. Later would come the younger men, and last the women and children. The heat entranced me. I sucked it deep into my lungs, where it warmed my vitals from the inside out; and I clambered to the highest bench where I sat moist and hot and glassy-eyed until my alarmed mother pulled me down and scrubbed me with soap and the fragrant cedar switches. The hardy would end with a plunge in the waters of the canal, which come directly from Lake Superior; others would content themselves with a sloshing rinse with water drawn by bucket from the end of the dock. At night, in bed and in my pajamas, I could still catch faintly the cedar smell on my skin.

What specifically drew my grandfather from Finland to Michigan's Upper Peninsula I never learned. Probably the life he left was so hard that anything would have seemed better. He was a farmer, but he had served in the Russian army, and my mother can remember him demonstrating the manual of arms with a broom. A brother had pre-ceded him to the new world, and apparently the news was good enough to persuade him to take the leap, probably about 1898. He left behind his wife and infant daughter, my oldest aunt, who would not be able to join him for several years. His brother went back to Finland, but my grandfather worked for a time in a Detroit factory before mak-ing his way to the north, where many Scandinavians had found a cli-mate and a landscape to remind them of home.

Upper Michigan's Keweenaw Peninsula stretches out northeast into Lake Superior in a long curving arm. It intercepts the winter winds dropping across the lake from out of Canada and accepts the burden of snow onto its forests and rocky hills, and onto the small fields cleared by the early farmers, eager to own land, who arrived at the turn of the century. It was a hard and bitter life, even for those raised in the harsh northland of the old country. Some winters the snows would accumulate to five feet or more. Each new snow would have to be shoveled higher along the paths from house to barn and outhouse; to care for livestock or to bring in firewood would be a confrontation with cheek-scalding wind from the lake; and trips to town would be by snowshoe or ski, or by horse and sleigh. Winter nights would be lighted by the vast flares and rolling curtains of the aurora borealis. By March the paths themselves would be packed feet deep in hard snow, and it would have been months since these farmers, their wives and children, had actually had their feet on the ground. Most of these farms are abandoned now, or reclaimed, a few of them, by hardy young people who value the isolation but who live by day jobs in town. These tend to be recent exiles from the cities further south. Many children of the first settlers left for jobs and easier lives down-state, or farther south still, as would my grandfather's children as soon as they were able. He had a small farm near the community of Salo for a while, where my mother was born and taken directly to the sauna for her first bath. I have walked those fields near Salo, in the few places between rock and swamp where it is possible to scrape in the earth and raise a little hay, feed a cow or two, coax along a few vegetables in the brief summers. But inevitably my grandfather was drawn into the copper mines in the years before the First World War. By that time he was already middle-aged.

Great veins of copper run through the rocky ridges of the Keweenaw Peninsula, and over one of them was developed the Quincy Mine. The operating capital, of course, came from investors in the East, and there has now been written an official history of the mine, which is long on the accomplishments of the investors and managers but short on the lives of the men who mined the ore. The mine had already a long record of intermittently profitable operations by the time my grandfather settled his family into a small company house just below the mine and began the grueling daily underground labor to see what profit he might wring from the rock. It must have been frighteningly unnatural work to begin so late in his life. As a farmer he had risen in dark and worked through the brightness of day to the night again, but now darkness claimed him the day round. The workday was twelve hours. In the winter, he would see daylight only on Sundays. The Finns were not originally miners; only the immigrants from Wales and Cornwall brought their profession with them, along with the Cornish *pastie,* the half-moon-shaped meat pie that could be heated in the morning and remain warm in the lunch pail until midday. The Finns soon adopted these along with their new work, and for twenty and more years my grandfather left each morning with his hot lunch pail for the climb up the hill to the Quincy Mine, to the daily descent into the pit.

It was brutal work. Only as my own body loses its resilience in middle age have I been able to imagine how brutal it must have been. From time to time the workers struck, of course: my mother's earliest memory was of abandoned lunch pails along Quincy Hill, where the violence of the 1914 strike intercepted those who tried to work before they could reach the mine. Sometimes a man would come home with his arm hanging limp, his shoulder dislocated from swinging a pick or sledge: a capable wife would put her man on the kitchen floor and, with one foot braced against his neck and the other against his armpit, pull and ease the shoulder joint back into place. Shafts would sometimes collapse, and the falling rock would shoot the compressed air out the opening of the mine shaft in a great air-blast heard in the homes below. And then the families would wait: my mother can remember lying with her ear to the basement floor, hoping to hear the miners hundreds of feet below. Other dangers came more slowly and insidiously. My grandfather wheezed with what was called miners' bronchitis, probably silicosis, that weakened him for the pneumonia that came in later years to kill him.

IV

How can I reconstruct his later life? The Quincy Mine closed in the Depression, a victim of declining demand and cheaper production from the open-pit mines of Montana and Arizona. Social Security was legislated in time to give him a small retirement income. In his entire life, he never drove an automobile, used a telephone, sent a telegram, or owned a radio. His Bible and the Finnish-language newspaper were his sole windows on the world. Most of his family and his wife's had remained in Finland, and now he was doubly isolated, for his children had married and left home, flowing into the mainstream of English-speaking life. He and my grandmother never learned English; the Finnish-speaking community was vital enough to hold them enclosed all their lives, and in the few photos they left I see the mark of the old world still on them. I never understood a word either of them ever said

My Finnish grandparents, circa 1926. ". . . I see
the mark of the old world still on them."

to me, except that my grandmother could approximate my name:
"*Veeli!*" she would call, "*Veeli boyga!*" I can still recognize the language
spoken, its unique rhythms and euphony of vowels, although it is
empty of meaning for me.

The talk during those summer visits surged back and forth between the two languages as my mother and my aunts deferred in turn
to their parents and to the children and husbands who spoke no
Finnish. Mostly we gathered for meals in the basement, which
became a summer kitchen with a door into the backyard. My grandmother was voluble and merry, but my grandfather would sit at one
end of the table, silent usually unless spoken to, while the conversation flowed mainly among the women in both languages. He was not
so much sunk in the silence of the listener or spectator as he was with-

drawn elsewhere. There is, some claim, a distinctive Finnish gaze, in which some Finns simply are not with you for a while, their eyes focused somewhere beyond on an inner horizon. At the furthest reaches of this gaze, I believe, is the music of Sibelius; and I suspect that it is in some dark way connected with the high incidence of suicide among Finns. My grandfather had it, as he drifted back, perhaps, beyond the long curve of the globe and the receding years, to some remote gatherings of family that had rooted themselves in his memory as these did mine. Returning, he would drink his coffee from his saucer, sometimes sucking it through a cube of sugar held in his teeth. It was the only indulgence I ever saw in his life.

Late in that summer a truckload of slab wood was dumped in the backyard, and in the afternoons he would split firewood to stove size and carry it into the basement to stack against the wall. My mother told me that by the time of cold weather he would have the basement filled from floor to ceiling with wood for the kitchen cookstove, the only heat the house would have. I sat one afternoon on the back steps watching him. He would balance the thin, wide piece of slab wood on the splitting block and with precise strokes of his ax reduce it to a few pieces of cookstove size, tossing them into a pile at one side. He gave no sign he knew I was there. I got out my pocketknife and began to whittle on one of the odd pieces of wood. It was a new knife, a few dimes extorted from my mother, with three blades and a celluloid grip in a swirl of blue, brown, and red. I thought it powerfully beautiful. Then I was aware of my grandfather standing over me, his dark hand thrust out. In the palm lay his knife—larger and ancient, it seemed, but with a handle in the same swirl of blue and brown and red. A smile cracked across his face, and there was a pattern of lines etched there I had never seen before.

For a moment we looked at each other, I still seated, he leaning on his ax, his other hand extended. Then he reached for a bushel basket nearby, picked up a few kindling chips from the ground around the splitting block, and motioned me to take over. After I had filled the kindling box in the basement, I helped him carry in the stove wood and stack it against the wall. Our work finished, we stepped together from the darkening basement into the chill twilight of the backyard. I felt a hand on my shoulder; his voice cracked and rasped.

"*Veeli,*" he said. "*Veeli boyga.*"

I never saw him again. We did not make a visit the next year; then the Second World War began, travel was restricted, and he died in late winter two years after. My grandmother followed him a few winters later. I remember the telegrams, the vacancy of my mother's absence for a week or so, the unintelligibility of a death so remote. Memories of my grandfather drifted to the margins of my consciousness for many years, except for a few provocations. I knew that he and I bore the same middle name. An older cousin once happened to remark that of all the cousins I most resembled him. And I remembered years earlier hearing her father say that my grandfather was, in his way, a very learned man, a lay scholar of the Bible—indeed, rising sometimes to dispute theology during the minister's Sunday sermon, to my grandmother's embarrassment, and, more recently, to my delight as my cousin tells the story. As the two observations coalesced, I felt a line of heritage begin to emerge, as I could find in him not only my name, my facial structure, my coloring, but also my love of the book and of the word, if not his faith in the Book and in the Word. And I never knew, until my wife told me, how characteristic were my moments of abstraction, when she would pass her hand between my gaze and my own inner horizon. But as the fullness of time brought me my children's children, I could feel him stalking nearer within me; and as I looked out over my own privileged life, I could look in more and more upon the bafflement, resignation, and consolations that must have been his. Now has age brought me full circle, to find my grandfather in myself as I seek myself in my grandson.

V

And so . . . forty-odd years after, I returned this summer to find that little frame house on the street rising up to the old mine. Curiously, I have had for more than a decade a summer cabin in the north, half a day from Hancock; but some unconfronted blockage in my thoughts prevented my return. It was, I finally understood, something I had been putting off for a long time. The house itself had been so altered by successive remodelings that at first I did not find it, but instead found the one next door, which was identical except that the floor plan was reversed: in it I met a man older than myself who remembered my uncle. No one was at home at the unrecognizable house next door, so I went on up the hill to the site of the Quincy Mine, now become a historical exhibit to attract tourists. One of which I was. And there I confronted, at a remove of two generations, something of the reality of that killing life of the hard-rock miner.

A pleasant young man guided our tour group from the gift shop into the hoist room, still housing the great steam hoist—the heart of the old Quincy operation and the glory of the present-day museum. It was a marvel of engineering in its day, and it remains impressive even now in its repose, towering three stories above the floor we stood upon. The guide's voice drifted away into the silence overhead, and I tried to imagine the din of this room years ago. Clanking and hissing as huge pressures of steam fed through its cylinders, the hoist turned a great double-coned drum that reeled and unreeled miles of steel cable through a tower-and-pulley system high overhead to the mine shaft itself, a hundred yards away. Here it was that my grandfather had gone underground, with others like himself, in small cars connected to the great hoist by the long and lengthening umbilical cord on which their lives depended. They dropped not straight down, as on an elevator, but down on rails at a steep angle into the hillside, the cable cars under controlled descent. Down they would roll in their little cars, leaning back against the slope as the cable lowered them a mile or more back down the hill they had just walked up to work, but now beneath the very houses in which they lived—there to attack the rock face with their drills and hammers and pickaxes, fighting off the dark with their carbide lamps and heaving the ore into cars that were hauled back up the track they had come down. The deeper shafts were baled of seeping water by special cars that scooped huge, dripping loads from the flooded chambers and discharged them at the mine head. At the end of the shift the men were retrieved, a more precious cargo, drawn back up the dripping shafts and delivered to the day, or night, to walk back down the hill to their homes below. Old photographs of the mining crews stare back at me from the museum walls: anonymous faces, sullen and apprehensive, of men young and in their middle age. I could not have recognized my grandfather had he been among them.

The abandoned shafts are inaccessible now, closed for safety, and much of the network of low tunnels and narrow chambers the miners groped through by their flaring lamps now lies dark and silent under tons of settled water. The older miners, like my grandfather, retired— grateful, no doubt, not to have to face the daily entombment that the old job entailed. The younger men drifted into different jobs or left town; and the town itself ceased to grow, declined, found a new sta- bility of a lower order, sustaining itself on tourists, a little lumbering, a growing college across the lake. No one's sons and grandsons would become miners, though, and no one's daughters would marry into the mines: my aunts and uncle and mother all left in time, finding their way to college and to jobs in the southern part of the state. The cop- per ore is still there, but too deep to be produced at a profit: thus to the slow fluctuations of economic law do I owe my own good fortune, not to have been a miner's son as well as grandson, and to have gone into the mines myself.

Further on up the peninsula is the older Delaware Mine, now open to the public—its first level only, saved from flooding by an under- ground stream that drains it. Down wooden steps at a steep angle we descend—a mere sixty feet or so—but the chill, the damp, the drip- ping rock, the smell of enclosed moisture drive into my bones a sud- den realization of what the grave must be. A string of dim lights lets the tourist see more clearly than the miners ever did the sloping cav- erns and narrow tunnels where they worked their days away. From one vantage point we can see the water flooding the levels below: a tossed pebble plunks into the dark water; ripples spread away into blackness. Our guide turns out the lights for a moment and jokingly gets us to see a ghost, some persistence on the retina of the vanished light. Other ghosts stir in me: in the flooded tunnels hundreds of feet below, here and at Quincy and at all the abandoned mines of this ancient and rocky land, ghostly miners toil slowly, like deep-sea divers in depths no one will ever see again, at one with rock and water and darkness. I begin to feel an old tightness in my neck and shoulders, a bursting of my lungs, as I strain upward and outward through dark, water-filled tunnels toward some light at the back of my mind. . . . Our guide turns on the light, and in a self-conscious shuffle our group begins the climb back to the surface, our claustrophobia palpable among us. We have been underground for twenty minutes. The chill is still deep in my body, and I think I understand what my grandfather sought to drive out with the fiercest heat of the sauna.

Later my wife and I found our way to the small cemetery on the hillside above the lake where my grandfather lay buried, my grandmother beside him. It was a hot day for Hancock; we sweated in our summer clothes. Part of the cemetery, the newer part, was neat and well tended—it had been endowed for perpetual care, the groundskeeper explained. The older section was overgrown and unkempt: formerly, families had tended the plots, but two generations had grown up and left the town, and there was no one to remember their dead. The groundskeeper consulted a rusty box of file cards and led us to the plot in his pickup truck; from the truck bed he pulled out a power mower and cut away the weeds and brambles over a small granite marker set flush with the earth. Names and year of death only. My oldest aunt had laid the marker, I assumed, the summer after my grandmother's death. To dig the winter ground is deadly hard work; even today, winter dead are stored for spring burial and brought to the cemetery, tiers of coffins on a flatbed truck, to be lowered into an earth become soft enough to receive them. My mother had never been able to visit the grave, so for her sake we took a picture. My wife borrowed a yellow rose from a nearby memorial basket and laid it across the stone.

Standing at his feet, feeling mortality tug at my bones, I thought of my grandfather lying still and patient in a chamber now too narrow to swing a pick in, waiting in sure and certain hope of the resurrection. The old dream flickers again behind my eyes, and for a moment he surfaces in my arms like a drowned man, I sink like one into his, and I am dreaming of my grandfather dreaming my dream. Deep beneath the earth, in dark, water-filled caves, we struggle upward together in tight embrace toward the day. . . . But as quickly as they coalesce the dreams diverge, and something has been exchanged. The dream of birth remains with him, and I am left with another I like less well. I stoop to return the rose to its rightful place. The summer sun is hot on my shoulders, but it does not reach deep enough to soothe a shudder at my heart.

V I

How those early days have marked me I understand only as I age. After my grandmother's death, my mother never returned to her childhood home. Always now she was reluctant to talk of the old times, and I can only guess how hard they must have been for her. In later years I have lived in California, in the Northwest, and in the South—but in time an inner compass asserted itself and I turned my face again and again to the north. A modest affluence and a profession neither of which my grandfather could have imagined permit me to spend my summers reading and writing in a summer home on a lake, where I have a leisure beyond his conception for the book and the word. But I do not spend my winters in this land. My daughter brings my grandson to visit on vacation. On my lap he will sit, turning pages of book after book with me; and I know that as he struggles toward words over bright pictures he will grasp a language that we share. The love of the book and of the word is grounded here. And I wonder what dreams from his childhood will connect him to me. Perhaps he will dream of great gray elephants swaying through rain-drenched pines and birch groves bathed in golden light. I dream now, from time to time, of dark passages, but I doubt that this is dream of birth.

The sun has passed from the lake, and as we sit in the gathering darkness voices fall silent and the evening chill descends on us. The first loon begins to call across the lake; another, more distant, replies. My grandson has clambered back up into my chair and lies sleeping against my chest; I have wrapped my arms about him against the cold, and we rest in one bonded warmth in the darkening night air. I am suddenly aware that my wife stands by my chair, puts her hand on my arm. "Why don't you start a fire?" she says. She takes the child from me with practiced grasp; he starts slightly, then sinks into deeper sleep. I stir myself to lay kindling in the fireplace, and soon the family drifts inside as the firelight leaps and glints about the room. I go outside for more wood where it is stacked in the crawl space beneath the porch: the fireplace is our only source of heat, and cutting and splitting firewood has become a ritual exercise—a recreation just so edged with necessity as to flavor the labor with both pleasure and virtue. No one, as yet, sits on the steps whittling with his pocketknife, waiting to gather chips. I gauge the size of the crawl space in my mind; it has never been filled, but a small person can stand upright in it and might get back into places too narrow for me to reach.

My arms loaded with wood, I pause to look out over the darkening lake. The loons are calling wildly now, from one end of the lake to the other; my heart leaps briefly out to them, then retreats as I turn back toward the cabin. For years we have talked of building a sauna. A friend has given me a makeshift stove, welded up from scrap metal, and I have plans for the building on paper. Perhaps I will stake it out next summer. There is plenty of firewood, and birch trees aplenty for the traditional birch switches. But I have my eye on a stand of white cedars just down the road, and as I turn back into the glowing cabin I wonder how much of the ancient heat I will be able to endure as I set the mark for those who will follow me.

Cradle Song, 1939

⁂

I WAS SEVEN YEARS OLD in the autumn of 1939, when the world began to open before me as a dark and troubling tunnel of time. For surely we enter time when memory divides from desire, when bliss drops away as loss, and hope and fear uncoil as one out of the timeless dream of infancy. Later comes the deeper perspective of age, when time before self becomes the matrix of history through which fate has forced its way, and time after self becomes . . . what? Another kind of matrix, perhaps, into which we project heart's desire in fate's stead, creating obligations beyond our grasp of days. In that autumn of 1939, as the great world beyond my ken shuddered on the verge of a great war, from over the horizon of history strode my Finnish grandmother, to lead me forward into the small world that lay no less incomprehensibly before me. Together we would wreak a tiny havoc to raise the deaf and the dead, and sing a charm against the world's terrors, great and small.

From the autumn of 1939, I remember this:

that Mrs. Harker would appear in our kitchen almost every afternoon, like some benign but befuddled presiding deity, to check on my mother as her pregnancy became more and more apparent. We were, after all, her tenants, at four dollars a week, in the little house just down the hill from her larger farmhouse. And she had

22

the telephone that would reach my father at the factory if this baby came in the night when he was away from home. We were, unavoidably, her dependents until this crisis was over.

As she left one afternoon she turned back to speak to my mother through the screen door. "Well," she sighed, "I really hope the mister is here to take you." Her broad face crinkled with concern. "I'll be glad to call the factory, of course, but Lord! I sleep like the dead, you know, and Frank is almost deaf as a post. Gabriel's trumpet wouldn't rouse him. If you have to go in the night, I don't know how you'll wake us up."

It was Indian summer. The maples in the woodlot beyond the fields flamed in slanting sunlight. Mrs. Harker's dog was pushing his nose through one of the holes in the tattered screen door. My little sister, Sylvia, was eating a doughnut and sharing alternate bites with the dog. My mother wiped her hands nervously on the apron stretched over her swollen front. Mrs. Harker, still talking, began to giggle as a new thought erased the worry. "Why, you know, one night last summer that old walnut tree went down right beside the house, took the screen right off our bedroom window, and put a branch right over our night table, and we neither one of us knew it till morning." Her face was now gleaming with mirth. "Frank was like to have a bird's nest in his hair when he rolled out that day."

My mother's smile was strained and embarrassed. My grandmother said something in Finnish. Doubly embarrassed, my mother had to translate; as an American child, she had early put the old language from her, and here, in the community she had married into, the tongue seemed outlandish. "She says, does your dog want a doughnut of his own . . . oh, dear!" She snatched the last of the doughnut as Sylvia took a bite; uncertain what to do, she pushed the last piece out through the hole to the dog.

Mrs. Harker opened her car door to let the dog in, then eased her bulk behind the steering wheel. My mother was trying to smile, but her face was tense. "Oh, I think Billy can wake you up. He's got a good voice."

My stomach was knotted with fear. All of this was pitched over my head, elliptical messages to keep me in ignorance. But I knew what was happening, what the future held. All I had to do, if my mother's baby

My home, 1938–1941. ". . . this decaying tenant house slumping into the ground."

came in the night, was to raise our sleeping benefactors from a death-like trance. Already I had been to one funeral, seen an uncle's silent body composed in stillness beyond our hushed voices, and now I pictured the Harkers, side by side in their matrimonial bed, embraced by great tree limbs and serenaded by singing birds, withdrawn into some deep evasion of Gabriel's horn and all the disasters of the world. Sometimes, I imagined, their dog slept with them too, sunk beyond all caring for doughnuts in some doggy oblivion of his own.

Already fear was my old friend: born, I know now, of my parents' fears as they sank in the collapsing world of the Great Depression. But I could not have named it then; at the time, it seemed simply the condition of my life. Already I could remember a succession of homes, sometimes with relatives, as my father drifted in and out of work; a succession of wheezing automobiles, abandoned or repossessed; a succession of friends briefly engaged and left behind with each move; until we had landed here, in this decaying tenant house slumping into the ground, with crazy tilting floors, crumbling plaster, and torn cheesecloth screens over cracked and gaping windows. It was four miles from town but with rent that we could afford.

Until that autumn of 1939, my grandmother had existed only as a foreshortened shadow in my consciousness. We had visited her, way in the north, once or twice, but I heard of her imminent arrival only with the passing visit of an older cousin from my mother's family. "She thought she'd better be on hand," he told my father as they sat sipping whiskey at the kitchen table. He had recently graduated from the School of Mines in the old hometown, had worked for a while in Venezuela, and was on his way to another job.

He had brought me a little jar of Mexican jumping beans. In the sunlight on the windowsill they would mysteriously twitch and quiver. Then he opened one of the beans with his knife and showed me the gnawing worm that devoured the bean from inside. From my fingernail it raised its head to me, then coiled and uncoiled in quest of the bed we had ripped it from. Somehow I was not surprised, and as I watched the remaining beans resume their slow dance in the sunlight the men talked of Hitler and the news from Europe. War was coming, I had heard many times. "He's got the Czechs, and now the Poles. Then he'll get France and England, and then we're next," my cousin declared, pouring more whiskey. I had seen Hitler once in a movie newsreel, heard his name again and again on the radio and running like a thread through the talk of the adults. He was connected in my mind with the man who had come one evening to our last house to take my father's car away. The man with the hook, my father said.

We had another car, now, though. Ten dollars down and the rest when they catch me, my father said. For now my father had a job on the night shift at the factory, twelve hours a night at forty cents an hour. These figures, like the rent sums, lodged in my memory like burrs until I was precocious in the arithmetic of poverty. Each evening after supper my father would drive the four miles into town, returning each morning after I had left for school. I rarely saw him except at supper and on Sundays. At breakfast I would sit in his chair as I ate my oatmeal. "You're the man in the family, now," my mother would say.

But they did not tell me about the coming baby. I could just barely remember a time when my sister had been presented to me, a visitor without warning. And of this one I knew nothing until I was told by Janet Castleman as we walked home from school. She was two grades ahead of me and had an older sister; already she was wiser in these matters than I would be for years, and she described in graphic detail the creature growing in my mother's body, how it had gotten there, and how it must come forth. Coming home, I saw with new eyes the swell beneath my mother's apron, a guilty secret that I was not supposed to know, and from then on I caught every guarded allusion that passed between my parents or flickered in the conversation of the women who visited from time to time. Some nights I was visited by a disturbing dream: in a tunnel of shapeless darkness, I was aware of a great throbbing worm somewhere beyond me, while the air about me crashed silently with unseen collisions.

In that autumn of fear I found two places of refuge, the school and the Harkers' milking barn; the road between them, half a mile either way from our house, marked the limits of my world. Every few days I would set off after supper with a covered gallon pail to bring home some milk; I would wait in the milking shed among the prowling cats and the quiet whoosh and crunching of the feeding cows while Frank Harker, crouched on the three-legged milking stool, squeezed the daily miracle of milk from the hanging udders into a pail. The air was rich with the scent of silage and hay and milk, warm with the creature comfort of animals, and I remember thinking that I would have liked to live right there in the barn. Frank Harker could not hear, and I simply waited until he noticed me, when he would grin and wink and, while the frantic cats rubbed against our knees, tip from his large pail a gallon into my little one. I would hand him the quarter my mother had entrusted to me; he would fumble in his overalls for his ragged coin purse and return to me a penny. School was my refuge every morning. It was a tumbledown place with one room, scarred double desks, and a rusted potbellied stove. The teacher was a middle-aged farmer's wife with the barest of credentials but with a good sense that bordered on wisdom. There I learned to play softball, and to read, and to sing. I had started the year before as a first-grader and had learned to read almost immediately, as though scales had simply fallen from my eyes. I was the youngest in a schoolroom of twelve, and by the end of the year I had sped with indecent precocity through all of my schoolbooks, and through most of those in the desks around me; and when Mrs. Hoff called the older students up to her desk to recite their lessons in history or geography, I listened intently to the stories of Squanto and the Pilgrims, of the great Emperor Charlie Main. I knew Checkle-slovakia on the map, and pondered the spelling and sound. Often I knew the answers to questions that the older students did not, and waved my hand furiously for attention. Wisely, Mrs. Hoff explained to me one day that my turn would come and others must have their chance first.

Wisely, too, she read stories to us at the beginning of each day— *Tom Sawyer, Huckleberry Finn, Pollyanna, The Secret Garden, Five Little Peppers.* I lived for those hours when stories rolled like controlled magic from the pages into my life; and on one memorable winter morning, sick with fever, I fought off my mother's concerns and stumbled my way to school to find out if Huck and Tom would succeed in freeing Jim from his bondage. Mrs. Hoff took one look at my flushed face and glazed eyes and brought me home in her car. The next week she let me read the chapters for myself, and when I finished she began to bring me books from the library in town. I was then for hours free in the consoling pages of books, but mopingly disconsolate at each necessary return to the world beyond their covers.

Softball and singing were our recreation. Twelve of us were just enough for a couple of short-handed teams at recess and at lunch hour, and by swinging furiously at gently lobbed pitches I would sometimes hit the ball sharply, sometimes get on base and score a run. We sang at the close of each day and when the weather kept us from softball, Mrs. Hoff pedaling vigorously at the old pump organ while we put our heads together over limp and tattered songbooks. Mrs. Hoff discovered in me a clear and true soprano and began to give me solo passages with a chorus of eleven throaty voices at my back. The game of softball I took home with me; from somewhere my father produced a ball and a bat, and with my sister as a fielder I tossed up the ball and launched tiny flies and grounders across the yard and ran miniature base paths until she tired of her duties and wandered away. My singing I kept to myself.

Sometime that fall my Finnish grandmother arrived from her home in the north, seven hundred miles away. We met her at the bus station, where she descended from the bus, a short pillar of a figure in black, chatting briskly to the driver. I could not understand what she was saying. The driver was grinning with incomprehension, but he cheerfully gave her a hand down and carried her bags to the sidewalk. "She's some lady," he said to my father as my mother embraced her and began to talk in a language alien to my ears.

I stood amazed at this new dimension in my life. Over my head a secret discourse was passing. "What are they saying?" I asked my father. "Beats me," he said. He ducked his head for a quick kiss and then gathered up her bags. Then she was enfolding me. I looked up to see a broad-cheeked, laughing face, wrinkled as a winter apple, and an expression so immediately familiar that it would haunt me for years. "*Veeli*," she said, "*Veeli boyga!*" "What is she saying?" I asked my mother desperately, pressed against the rough wool coat.

"That's your name," she said. "Billy. Billy-Boy."

I hated it. As we walked to the car, my father leading with the bags, my mother bearing her open secret beneath her open coat, my grandmother carrying Sylvia, I followed behind, writhing in outrage and betrayal.

My grandmother, I have since learned, was a great voyager. My grandfather had emigrated first, and when he had earned a little money he sent it to her for her passage. The first stage of her journey was from Finland to Liverpool, where she remained some time awaiting further passage: twenty-four years old, a farm girl with a child in arms, alone in that foreign city. Once she had reached the little mining town in northern Michigan, no travel daunted her. With no English and with little money, she would in later years launch herself out by train or bus to visit her distant children, trusting to the goodwill of conductors or drivers, to the kindness of strangers, and to her own native wit to bring her to her destination. She was merry and voluble; that she was seldom understood never prevented her from talking to anyone. My grandfather, who had made the one voyage of his life, remained at home. I cannot guess what had passed in letters from my mother to my grandmother, but now she had found a need and had come to serve it. The black coat and dress were hung away, and in a faded housedress, an apron damp from dishwater, a kerchief and flopping felt slippers, she took over our home.

The new language took over our home as well. My father, during his few hours with us, kept largely silent as my mother and grand-mother talked and talked. Sylvia began to prattle in Finnish phrases, to my grandmother's great delight. My grandmother talked to me often, and hugged me to her damp bosom; her gaze seemed to hold a secret for me, but the language sealed me off from the new life of the family. At about this time, I got a library card from the library in town. Each Saturday, when we went to town to buy groceries, I could get two books. Then I got a card for my sister, who could not read, and I could get four books. I retreated to the silence of the printed page and let the flow of Finnish roll by me like a river past an island.

But I could not read always. Once, as summer lingered in the short afternoon of an October day, Sylvia and I were playing soft-ball. By now she had developed a rudimentary sense of justice and insisted on being allowed to bat, so I would station her against the pump-house wall and lob balls at her bat until a weak fly or bunt dribbled off. I would grab it and tag her before she could run a base, then she could resume chasing balls for me until her sense of justice welled up again. I looked up to see my grandmother bearing down on us, grinning broadly and speaking Finnish. I bounced a pop fly off Sylvia's bat and caught it against my chest. "You're out," I shout-ed, and she dutifully trotted out to field.

My grandmother picked up the bat and held it in a batting stance. She wanted to play with us. Perplexed, I began to lob balls toward her; again and again she swung stiffly. Then, surprisingly, she got a solid hit. It struck me thump in the stomach, but some-how I held on. "Out!" I called. "You're out!" I took the bat out of her hands.

She took the ball and launched an awkward pitch toward me. It went over my head; the next one hit me in the ankle. She could throw harder than I could. She was laughing and so was Sylvia, and even my mother came out from the kitchen to lean her tired back against the clothesline post and watch us. My grandmother pitched the ball again and said something to my mother. "Come on, throw straight," I shouted.

"She says, back in Finland she used to throw stones at the cows, bringing them home from pasture," my mother said.

Ball after ball came at me erratically, and I began to swing viciously at anything I could reach. I wanted to drive the ball far over their heads, trot the bases triumphantly while Sylvia pursued the ball down the driveway to the road. Finally I caught one and sent a pop fly spinning overhead. As I stood watching, my grandmother stepped forward, held out her apron, and caught the descending ball. Her face glowed with smiles. "Out!" she called, laughing. "Out, *Veeli boyga!*" Sylvia came bounding in from the field; she knew the rules. "You're out!" she shouted. "My bat! My bat!"

I was murderous with rage. I threw the bat wildly across the fence. My grandmother looked puzzled. I stood in front of her and shouted as loudly and slowly as I could: "DAMMIT! SPEAK ENGLISH! WHY DON'T YOU SPEAK ENGLISH?"

As the year dragged on through November we began to prepare for the Thanksgiving Day program at school. We decorated the walls and windows with artwork and penmanship. From each home we collected vegetables and canned goods to make up a basket for a door prize. There would be a little play and some recitations. Finally there would be a choral presentation in which I would sing a solo. For weeks we practiced daily, and Mrs. Hoff rehearsed me in my lyrics until I knew them perfectly. "Now, you don't need to be afraid," she cautioned me. "Just don't look at anybody in the audience. You just look straight at the back wall, right at the top of the windows, and sing just like you do every day."

The program was scheduled for the night before Thanksgiving. My father was at work, but my mother and my grandmother and Sylvia walked the short half mile to the schoolhouse. Assembled were twenty or so parents and babies, crowded into our desks and squeezed onto the benches beneath the coat hooks at the rear. Behind a black baize curtain strung on a wire across the teacher's platform we prepared each performance, then huddled silently while the two tallest students drew back the curtains. My solo would be last, followed by group singing and the door prize.

Before the most tolerant audience in the world we limped, shuffled, and stumbled through our paces. Then with Mrs. Hoff at the organ, we sang a medley of songs. The time had come for my solo. Mrs. Hoff struck a chord, and all twelve of us hummed our way through a melody that everyone in the room knew. Then, two steps forward, eyes fixed on the corner above the window, I began to sing:

> If you were the only girl in the world,
> And I were the only boy,
> Nothing else would matter in the world today,
> We could go on loving in the same old way . . .

Although I did not know it, the song had been made popular by Rudy Vallee in a movie, *The Vagabond Lover,* and it had been on the radio for years. For me it was simply my song, perfect in its own inner logic and unchanging each time I came back to it. I could hear my voice ringing out over the assembled heads; doggedly I fixed my eyes on the distant wall, but slowly my gaze drifted to where my mother and grandmother sat, Sylvia on my grandmother's lap. My grandmother was smiling proudly, but my mother sat as if transfixed. She had heard me sing with the radio and with my father, but never like this, never in public.

> If you were the only girl in the world,
> And I were the only boy . . .

The first verse was ended. I stood silently, looking at my mother; the rasping chorus hummed again through the melody. I sang once more:

> A garden of Eden, just made for two,
> With nothing to mar our joy.
> I would say such wonderful things to you,
> There would be such wonderful things to do,
> If you were the only girl in the world,
> And I were the only boy.

I quavered on to the end, a piping vagabond lover, but my mother had dropped her eyes to the floor. There was applause as I stepped back into the chorus, then group singing, and my grandmother won the door prize.

The winter moved toward December with deepening cold but no snow. The rutted mud of the road congealed into permanent ridges and folds, iron-hard beneath my feet as I walked back and forth to school. The thermometer dropped toward zero, and during the day we abandoned all the rooms of the house but the kitchen with its hot and glowing range. Firewood was stacked near the back door and in the wood box behind the range; and from town my father brought a small trailer full of coal that we used to keep the fire over until morning. And one night my grandmother peered out of the north window and said something excitedly to my mother. We put our coats on and huddled on the back step, looking up at the northern sky where huge shifting folds of pale light flickered along the horizon. My grandmother was talking quietly. "What is it?" I asked.

"The Northern Lights," my mother said. "We don't usually get them this far south. They covered the sky the night your grandmother left Finland. She left in a sleigh pulled by two horses, under a sky of white fire, she says." The next night, as we sat in the kitchen listening to the radio, I looked up from my book to see my grandmother's face streaked with tears; she was murmuring in a broken voice. Reading, I had paid no heed, but my mother had been translating from the radio broadcast. Russian troops had invaded Finland.

My mother spent more and more time sitting in her rocking chair in these last days, legs spread beneath the mound of her belly. I had long since forsaken her lap, but Sylvia still clambered up, seeking purchase where there was little room. She seemed to understand Finnish now, following my grandmother's bidding and even my mother's in that language. My mother seemed to have sunk back into the language of her childhood; she spoke English to me, but with an effort, it seemed, and I retreated more and more into my books each day after school. Only when Mrs. Harker stopped by did our household language revert to English. *Meesis Hockkeri,* my grandmother called her as my mother translated their chatter. I could sense the relief when she left. We were all waiting.

When my mother awoke me that night I knew before she said anything that the time had come. All she said was, "You'll have to go and wake up Mrs. Harker. Grandma will go with you. Pound on the door as hard as you can. Call under her window until she wakes up. Call as loud as you can."

My grandmother was already in her black coat and a heavy shawl. I pulled my school clothes on over my pajamas. Together we set out toward the Harkers'. From the south, moonlight washed from a cloudless sky over the frozen land, while in the north the great lights flared and surged again from the horizon. We could see as though it were day, but it was deathly cold; even the faint wind was sharp against my face. The Harkers' cow barn loomed at the curve of the road; beyond it the windmill marked the dooryard of the house. My grandmother stumbled slightly in the rutted road and clutched at my hand. "*Veeli boyga,*" she said, and then something else to me. I pulled away and ran up the road ahead of her. I was already at the Harkers' back door, hammering with mittened fists and calling, when my grandmother labored up, breathing heavily. "Mrs. Harker! Mrs. Harrr-ker!"

My voice floated feebly up toward the flaring lights in the sharp night air. The door was heavy, solid, and barely sounded beneath my padded blows. There was no answer from the darkened house. I began again, and behind me my grandmother's voice chimed with my own. "*Meesis Hock-keri,*" she called. "Mrs. Harker!" I shouted, pounding at the door until my fists ached. The silence between my cries stretched into an eternity.

I ran around to the front of the house, beneath the Harkers' bedroom window, and began to call again. My grandmother followed after me. We called alternately and in cacaphonic unison:

"Mrs. Harrr-ker!"

"*Meesis Hock-keri!*"

"Mrs. Harker!"

"*Meesis Hock-keri!*"

There was only silence from the house, and I was sobbing with fear and frustration. I turned angrily on my grandmother. "Shut up!" I screamed. "If you can't speak English, just SHUT UP!"

I faced the house again and searched desperately for my loudest voice. I took a deep breath, and unbidden the song floated up into the winter night:

> If you were the only girl in the world,
> And I were the only boy . . .

My grandmother stared at me as I sang. Then with a quick movement of her heel she kicked up a whitewashed stone from the frozen flower bed beneath the window; with a stiff underhand pitch she tossed it up toward the window just a few feet above our heads.

The stone rattled harmlessly off the clapboards and fell at my feet. I grasped the stone and the idea in one instant. The missile was no larger than my tiny fist; I flung it with all my strength toward the glass above. The window shattered magnificently in the stillness of the night, and in the quiet moment that followed I found another voice released from some obstructed passageway in my angry heart. My grandmother had turned her face up to the broken window and was calling again. *"Meesis Hock-keri!"* I took her hand and raised my voice in unison with hers. *"Meesis Hock-keri!"* we called together, blending a boy's treble and an old voice from the old country, trying with one mingled tongue to wake the deaf and the dead. *"Meesis Hock-keri!"* But it was Mr. Harker whose astonished face appeared at the hole overhead and who let us in at the kitchen door, still wearing his nightshirt and still holding the whitewashed rock that had broken into his night. Mrs. Harker's dog was nosing at her bare ankles as she cranked up the operator on the telephone on the kitchen wall.

A half hour later my father was home for my mother and gone again, and while I slept and the night sky flared in enigmatic signs, my brother Roger was born, coming home the week before Christmas. The credit and the blame for the broken window went entirely to me, but whether by my grandmother's story or by simple mistake I could never tell. I was, for the moment, a tiny hero, willing to believe what was believed of me, while my grandmother in her wisdom said nothing. "Lordy," Mrs. Harker chortled, "no great harm done, and he did just what he had to do." As we traveled the winter road back and forth to town, the large cardboard patch in the Harkers' bedroom window proclaimed my fame. In the spring, my father bought new glazing, and he and I together went to repair the damage of that perilous night.

As that winter deepened, my mother grew back into her strength and reassumed control of our house. My grandmother let her work, while she sat long hours holding and rocking my new brother. "*Rotcheri,*" she called him, "*Rotcheri boyga,*" and that became his name among us, as easily on my tongue as on hers. As she rocked, she crooned a simple melody in strange rhyme:

> Piun, paun! Paukkaa!
> Janis metsässa laukkaa:
> Kili, kili kellot kaulässa;
> Peipin housut naulässa.

The melody and its language, the rhythm of the rocking chair, set the song fluttering in my throat. "What does it mean?" I asked my mother. She smiled vaguely. "It's just nonsense," she said. "Like this."

> Bells sound! Bushes crack!
> Through the woods The Rabbit comes:
> Ringing bells around his neck;
> While baby's pants on a nail are hung.

Outside, the deep cold had broken and the still and milder air was thick with gently falling snow. It settled slowly through the evening sky in dimly luminous undulations, brightening the dusk against the coming night. Already the leafless woods across the field were edged in white in every line against the darkening horizon, and the frozen and corrugated earth was softened under a mantle of white. I leaned my forehead against the cold glass of the north window. Somewhere a great rabbit was leaping from drift to drift, strange bells ringing faintly through the silent woods. Somewhere Finnish soldiers lay concealed in snow, facing an advancing Russian army.

My grandmother was preparing Roger for his bath in front of the kitchen range. She stuffed the firebox with wood until the kitchen was heavy with heat and drew the kitchen table close to the stove. She bathed him gently in the dishpan, then laid him naked on a towel on the table. He twitched and squirmed and turned his head blindly from side to side; then from the tiny penis shot a quick golden stream that popped and sizzled as it sprayed across the surface of the hot stove. My grandmother laughed uproariously. As the baby began a faint, choking cry, she deftly diapered him, tugged him into a nightgown, and gave him to my mother to nurse. The searching mouth found the breast and fell silent save for a muffled, liquid sound.

Later, the nursing done, my mother placed him on the table again for another change of diaper. My grandmother had turned the lamp down low; only a small circle of light held the table centered in the shadows of the surrounding room. My brother lay quietly, dark eyes open, searching from face to face as we bent over him. My grandmother said something in Finnish, pushed me into the rocking chair, and laid the wakeful bundle in my arms. "She says you should rock him now," my mother said.

Time had uncoiled and had delivered the future into my arms. My brother's eyes swept the circle of light, caught and held my face. My feet did not reach the floor, so my grandmother rocked the chair from behind. In a sudden upwelling my voice found all the Finnish I would ever learn. "Piun, paun! Paukkaa!" I sang quietly into the darkening room:

> Janis metsässa laukkaa:
> Kili, kili kellot kaulässa;
> Peipin housut naulässa.

As I sang, over and over to the rocking of the chair, my brother drifted into sleep, while the song in its simple and perfect logic became for the moment a stay against the terror that had wrapped itself around the world.

Plenitude

I NEVER KNEW MY FATHER'S FATHER, who died the year I was born. He had come to this country as a young man from Lübeck, Germany, and I know nothing of his early life. He found my grandmother, seven years younger and American born, in the German farming community of our county, but the language in the family was always English. Early photographs show a strikingly handsome man, bearded and mustachioed, posed proudly with his robust, rawboned wife and their growing family. He worked in a lumberyard and in a furniture factory most of his life; from my remaining uncle, who like all his family seems to have little interest in the past, I can retrieve only that my grandfather once pulled a live mouse by the tail from his tin of chewing tobacco, and that he always put food on the table for his eleven children. For me, the family was always defined by my grandmother, who outlived him by twenty-three years and was the center of a complex, active family life while I was growing up. I knew her as she aged from her sixties into her eighties, a genial bulk of a woman slow of movement and quick to laugh. Her accomplishment had been to bear and raise the eleven, a new face, mouth, and name every two years, diapers for a quarter century, until she was decommissioned by menopause. A family photograph shows ten of them in stairstep order, my

Ten of the eleven children in my father's family, circa 1914, "my father
. . . next to last and in slightly blurred motion."

My Aunt Caroline, who was not born at
the time of the family stairstep photo.

father at age four next to last and in slightly blurred motion; his youngest sister, my Aunt Caroline, I calculate to have been an imminent eleventh in utero behind the camera; and already I can see that my book cannot be big enough to contain this family.

By the time that I can remember, the several sisters and brothers had mostly all moved out, married, and begun families of their own, save my youngest aunt, who lived as companion to my grandmother even after she was married and raising children herself. I was the twenty-first grandchild in a series that eventually reached forty-two. The number comes from my grandmother's obituary: my count cannot muster so many, but my memory is hazy regarding some much younger than myself. No one moved far away; our small town swarmed with my cousins, and most weekends we visited one or two families as well as my grandmother, or they visited us.

The distinguishing feature of this clan must certainly have been its numbers: a family story tells that when one of my cousins was subject to a background check for an Army security clearance, the investigating officers encountered first his brother and then a cousin before finding someone who was not a relative. When I was a kid, a car from South Carolina pulled up beside me downtown, somebody passing through, looking for an old Army buddy—who was, of course, one of my cousins just down the street. Years later, a college friend, trying to find me, called the switchboard at my hometown, where the operator put her in touch with my Aunt Marguerite, who walked down to my mother's house to get my number. And this family's second distinction must have been its sheer ordinariness: before me, only one cousin had gone to college; and only my brother Roger and two or three others ever went to jail, and only one to a mental institution. Most lived and worked contentedly in the middle ground, factory workers most of them, marrying and baptizing and burying in the Lutheran church, and singularly incurious about anything outside the family circle.

My oldest aunt, Edna, perhaps achieved some distinction by marriage, as did my youngest aunt, Caroline. The engineer Edna married became mayor of our town for a few years, and their oldest son was in law school until the war, when he died in a plane crash. Caroline's husband became a factory manager after my grandmother died and he could leave town to follow his opportunities. Two of my aunts I never knew, I was so young when they died, but the rest remained the cast of characters for the weekly family drama of visits, eating, and endless, endless talk. It was years before I knew their proper names, because most went by a nickname or sometimes two, in a family code that outsiders, or in-laws new to the family, despaired of learning. Edna, severe and straight, had none that I knew of, but next oldest to Edna was my Uncle Bing, whose real name was Albert; he rose to be a factory foreman and, as an amateur barber, gave me many haircuts for the usual fee of a bottle of beer, one of six or so that my father would bring to share with whatever other family members were at hand. Next to Albert was James Frederick, or perhaps Frederick James, since either name might be used when he was not called Fritz; he was in the factory too, but on Sundays he dressed like a banker, and with a cigar and a resonant voice he was the most distinguished-looking man I knew; he and Albert were both conscripted as young men in the First World War but saw no action. Edith and Rose died before I knew them, stricken young by cancer, but Rose's husband, Roy, was called the Rabbitshooter. If John had a nickname I have forgotten it, but Freda was called Katy and sometimes Morrie. My Aunt Marguerite with the wooden leg was called both Ollie and Min; she was married to my Uncle Dingy, whose real name was Henry, but that sobriquet remains so delicious that to this day I cannot give it up. My father was Cedric and my Uncle Ray was Ignatz, and my Aunt Caroline was alternately Charlie or Toppy. My grandmother remembered them all, as well as the given names of her grandchildren, but this renaming did not extend to my generation. Somehow, invention had flagged.

II

Troubles came and went without damping the cheer. My Aunt Marguerite was a little girl when she lost her leg. On the way to a church Christmas service one night with her sisters, she caught her foot in the railway tracks at a crossing. A train was bearing down; her sisters pulled her to one side and held her in their arms while the train took off her foot above the ankle; subsequent surgery left her a stub below the knee. As the story goes, her father buried the foot in a tin box in the backyard. As she recovered, she cried at the phantom pain of the missing toes, and her father dug up the foot and unclenched the dead toes, hoping to ease her pain. She was the most cheerful woman I knew, walking with only a slight limp. She had to go to Grand Rapids every few years to have a new leg fitted, and when she returned she got out of the car with her old leg under her arm and stored it up on the rafters of my grandmother's garage. I remember gazing up at a series of them hanging overhead, dusty and cobwebbed in graduated sizes from a tiny original, and I often wonder now where they have gone, and what god-awful emergency they might have been saved for. When I was little, sitting at her feet, she would make me guess which was the wooden leg. She wore hose, so I couldn't tell without thumping both in comparison; and then, pulling a pin from her collar, she would look at me with wide eyes and thrust the pin into the leg I had identified. "None of your other aunts can do that!" she would announce, laughing; and my Uncle John would claim that my father had a wooden butt from driving truck so long, and ask for the pin to test it, and my father would threaten to test John's wooden head, and my Aunt Freda, whose humor ran to the bawdy, whispered something to Caroline, then young and unmarried, who blushed and would not repeat what she said, but Freda's husband, Uncle Ernie, had heard, and said that if that was true there wouldn't be so many children around, but the women would be happier. Marguerite's husband, Uncle Dingy, was missing the two middle fingers of his left hand, from a sawmill accident some said, but others said he had really blown them off with a shotgun, hunting while drunk, or that a bulldog had mauled them. Uncle Dingy was a painter, and the paint can hung in his left hand from two hooked fingers; with them and his thumb he could also grip a beer bottle with great dexterity. I have wondered if he and my aunt were drawn together because of their missing body parts, and why, of all the family, they had no children.

My Aunts Edith and Rose I knew only by the families they left after their deaths. Edith's husband, my Uncle Dewey, was my Uncle Dingy's older brother; he and Edith had five boys under fifteen and a little girl who died from eating rat poison. I remember visiting them once, in a dim and fetid house on a dirt street near the edge of town; Edith lay in her bed in a downstairs room and my cousins and I sat quietly in the living room while my parents went in to see her. She died the summer my father was out of work and we lived in the front parlor of my Aunt Freda's house. Dewey could not manage five boys, so as my family moved out to the little house in the country, the two youngest boys moved in with Freda and Ernie and their five children. Teddy, the youngest, was just my age, and Freda said that he was crusted with dirt, scabby with sores, and infested with head lice. He and I went through high school together, two more different cousins not to be imagined—I the driven achiever; he the cheerful underachiever. He wore no underwear because he said it made too much laundry—this was after Dewey had remarried and taken the two youngest back in with him. We were both on the football team; Teddy got a bloody nose every day and left his mark on everyone's practice jersey until the coach in disgust sent him to the team doctor to have his vein cauterized. Later he went into the Navy and then worked in the factory, and he missed my last class reunion because he was at a reunion of his battleship. His next older brother became a fireman and lately has taken to restoring furniture, having redone some cane chair seats for my mother-in-law. The oldest brother once came to visit us in the country riding a motorcycle; my father called it a puddle jumper and got on and rode it around the yard under the pine trees, laughingly offering his collapsing '29 Chevy in trade. The three older boys went to live with my grandmother and my Aunt Caroline, who raised them until each successively finished high school and joined the Navy, when they sent back gifts of exotic silk pillows and carved lamps and curios from far-flung ports.

Rose's family of four broke up similarly a few years later, except that their father, the Rabbitshooter, simply walked out and left them after Rose's death. The oldest boy and girl went to live with my Aunt Edna, whose sons were both in the military—this was during the war, of course. The youngest boy and girl went also to my grandmother and Caroline, but the first batch of Edith's boys were all out and in the Navy by then. My grandmother and Caroline raised this second family through high school as well. The Rabbitshooter was in turn abandoned by his children, who would have nothing to do with him. In later years I would see him downtown, a bleary drunk in dirty overalls; he died a pauper, demented, unvisited, unlamented in a nursing home.

All of these abandoned children finished high school, none went to college, none went to jail. My grandmother saw nothing extraordinary in all of this: before my time, she had taken into her family of eleven two boys from the neighborhood in a time of distress.

I I I

My own family passed through this network of care as well. In the early years of the Depression, my father's work was intermittent and unreliable. As the birth of my sister drew near, we left our apartment in Detroit and my mother and I moved into my grandmother's house with her and Caroline; Aunt Marguerite was not yet married to Dingy and lived there as well. I was three when my sister was born, and my mother went to my Aunt Edna's for recovery, where there was a downstairs bedroom, and then the three of us remained at my grandmother's for the summer, my father visiting intermittently as his truck route took him through town, after which we went north to live with my mother's family for a year. But in my grandmother's house that summer, I was a great favorite with my unmarried aunts, who took up some of the vacancy I felt in my mother's attention to me. Both Caroline and Marguerite worked in the office of a nearby factory, and I would walk to the street corner at five o'clock to meet them, sometimes with matches I had stolen from the kitchen to light for my amusement. At the other end of the street was a park that I liked to run off to, until my Uncle Ray told me there was a wolf down there that would bite my weenie off, which gave me bad dreams for a while. Once a week or so my father would pass through with a load of new cars on his truck and park in front of the house; they were my father's cars, I was told with many laughs, but I was not told why we did not have one. Through the house all of the family passed constantly in a parade of talk and laughter and meal after meal at my grandmother's long table. Generally there was fried chicken, from the penned flock in the backyard; she kept chickens every year well into her old age, except the one spring the chicks all died save one, which she named Puny and kept as a pet. Her five sons gave her a canary, which she named Albert Frederick John William Raymond, and that summer they gathered to fill the old cistern with rocks and dirt and then to build a rock garden and a goldfish pond in her backyard, in the hole excavated to fill the cistern. I have a picture of me fishing in the pond, and I did fall in once, only to be rescued by Aunt Caroline. They also poured a new patch of sidewalk at the end of the driveway and pressed my bare feet into the wet cement, adding my initials and the date. For years I could walk by and find my past ratified in the impress of tiny feet.

Three years later we fell on the family bounty again. We had lived for a year in a little bungalow out by the railroad tracks and the gasworks; I had gone to kindergarten nearby, and I had friends at each end of the street—a boy who once shot me in the head with an arrow (fortunately blunted) and who later went to jail for murder, and another boy whose dim and grimy house terrified me with its silence; his father was later sentenced for incest with his daughters. We had a vegetable garden in the backyard where I picked carrots, but when my father lost his job and the man with the hook came for his car and we could not pay the rent we had to leave; a few weeks later, when we returned to visit neighbors, I went to the garden and pulled an armload of vegetables—the new renters, I imagine now, were not at home. We had moved by then into the home of Aunt Freda and Uncle Ernie, who gave us the front parlor to live in. All but one of their five children were older than I was, and their neighborhood I found of vital interest. Next door lived a woman my aunt said had dyed hair and whom my father called a grass widow; as she and her boyfriend sat in their car in the evenings, the older boys would creep up and rock the bumpers. She had two boys whose chief achievement was to bite worms in half; when she came over to show off her pearl-and-sapphire engagement ring the ladies all admired it, and when she left my father said that at last she was an honest woman, almost. Down the street was a one-eyed boy with a patch over his eye, where his brother had hit him with a dart; later, in grade school, he had a glass eye that he would take out and roll around his desk. Across the street lived municipal judge Theo Jacobs, called Jug Jacobs by all the kids and my father, who had a terrifying Great Dane barking in his backyard. At the corner was the Paris Bakery, where I would be sent on Saturday mornings for a bag of sugar cookies because the lady there had a crush on me, called me her little sugar cookie, and gave me fourteen or fifteen to the dozen. My Uncle Ernie was a painting contractor who every ten years painted our church at cost and once showed us four bushels of old chewing gum he had scraped off the seat bottoms of the Strand Theater; that summer he spread some of his great canvas drop cloths over the clotheslines to make tents for my cousins and me to play in; we set up a mock store to sell drinks, but all we had to sell was sugar water, salt water, a mixture of the two, and one with pepper added, and soon we were all sick from our wares. In the garage we made hydrogen gas from muriatic acid in a beer bottle, into which we dropped bits of zinc broken off canning-jar lids; a balloon stretched over the neck of the bottle filled with gas, and we would tie notes to it and send it aloft, but no messages were ever answered. Soda bottles broken down to just their circular bottoms became crude magnifying glasses, focusing the sun's rays so we would sizzle to death ants and worms and captured grasshoppers, or build newspaper fires in the alley. On the Fourth of July we made crude bombs by biting off match heads, stuffing ten or a dozen into a nut on a one-inch bolt, another bolt then screwed in tight to make an explosive chamber; when thrown hard against the pavement, it would explode with a satisfying crack, sending a bolt high into the trees. Jake Jordan put a stop to it; he was the town motorcycle cop, on a white Harley in the days when the Lone Ranger was a popular radio program, and whenever he rolled by we would run along the sidewalk after him, shouting, "Hi-Yo Silver! Awa-a-a-y!" We practiced our Johnny Weissmuller Tarzan yells up and down the block and swung on a rope from the back porch. My oldest cousin cut out toy pistols from old boards for us on my uncle's jigsaw and bored out a finger hole at the trigger and a barrel hole at the business end; one evening on the back porch my Aunt Freda picked up one of these guns, handed it to my father, and asked him to smell the barrel. "Do you know what you just smelled?" she laughed. "That's Charlie McCarthy's asshole!" My father immediately went over and pulled the joke on the grass widow's bridegroom in the backyard next door, and when I pulled it on my mother she took the gun away from me. We lived there only three months, but I have never felt so much a part of a family.

There was only one other death that I recall in those years. My

Uncle John's little boy died of influenza, and when we went to visit them my Aunt Katherine could not stop crying. Later she had another little boy who lived; she named him James after his dead older brother, to the scandal of the rest of the family, who thought no good would come of it, that he would be haunted, but after all, she was a Wiedemann, she had married into the family, and what could you expect? And no good did come: haunted or not, he was in and out of jail later, an embarrassment to my younger brother James, who did not go to jail but who carried the same name, which was not unusual in my family—several cousins shared first and last names and were usually separated by their parents' names—John's James as distinct from Freda's James or Bill's James, who was called Mike within the family, usually. My Uncle John had enlisted in the Army after the Great War and had served in Hawaii. He was a hard worker, usually with two jobs and part-time ventures; he cut wood in the winter with my father, and when we moved to the country he raised potatoes on rented land down the road; one cold November night we all picked potatoes by automobile headlights to beat a freeze; and later, when we had moved to town, he would sometimes pitch stolen boards out the factory window into our backyard to retrieve for his projects. John was the great reader in the family; once I learned to read, he lent me his cardboard box full of all the Tarzan books, and all summer, the summer we kept his dog Spot, I crept through tall grass on the spoor of imaginary African game. He told me that when he was a kid, he had belonged to a Tarzan club; they had crept out of the house at night and met at Kelly's Woods, where they would build a bonfire, dance naked, and swing on wild grapevines; the leader was the son of Reverend Schalm, our church pastor, who later became a veterinarian. The son, I mean.

My cousin Freddie did not die, but he was odd from childhood on, and even by the time he was grown, a strapping young man, he still looked like a baby, with a big, mooning face and a childish grin. He was my Uncle James's only son, and my parents always said he was like that from being raised with a family of girls, but I think he was really schizophrenic, which we did not know about in those days. He saw a lot of movies as a kid, and he always identified people by the movie stars they resembled. Young and chubby, I was Charles Laughton; later, grown, I became Jimmy Stewart. Freddie was silly in school, just a year behind me, and an embarrassment because he carried my family name. Eventually he fell into ungovernable rages, threatening his father, and was put into the state hospital in Kalamazoo; lately I have heard that he has been released into the care of a foster family. One of his sisters has published a supermarket romance novel that I have not read; her sister, who I met at my mother's funeral, says that she is at work on one also, set in Georgian England, and I wonder if my literary bent, always identified with my mother's family, might come covertly from this other strain. Freddie's mother was famous in our family for her fear of thunderstorms; Uncle James worked nights, and when thunder and lightning threatened, she took her children all to her mother's, where they would be safe, she said. She was silly, of course, but she had married into the family; she was a Middlestadt, and what could you expect?

There was little notable about the rest of the family. My youngest uncle and aunt, Ray and Caroline, both married within my memory. Caroline married late for our family, probably missing most suitors because she was so obviously obliged to stay with my grandmother. But along came Charlie, who saw her virtues, and once married they were Charlie and Charlie, not to be confused with my brother Charlie or my cousin Charlie or a great-uncle Charlie. Caroline's Charlie was the quietest, most patient man I have known, living a decade and more in his mother-in-law's house and driving fifty miles round-trip to work each day. My Uncle Ray I remember being teased by my father about the young woman from Indiana he was seeing; flustered, he said he was going to ditch her. A few months later the pair made their ritual trip from family to family announcing their engagement, with cigars and whiskey for the men, candy for the children; and buoyed by the teasing banter, I shouted, "Uncle Ray, I thought you said you were going to ditch her." My mother took me by the hair into the kitchen and isolated me for the evening, but I seem to have done no harm, as they are married still. As is my cousin Charlie, or was until he died lately, who, when he went off to the Army, left behind a girlfriend who showed up at his mother's house wearing an engagement ring and planning a wedding on his safe return. His mother knew nothing of all this, nor did Charlie, according to his letters; but he returned safely and married the girl anyway and seemed to live happily ever after.

In my father's family of eleven marriages there were no divorces and, so far as family gossip goes, no infidelities. My generation has been less steady, but the failures have been rare.

IV

The Second World War was the defining world event during my years growing up in this family. I was too young to go, and my father and his brothers were too old, but my older cousins went during and some afterward, more or less on family momentum. All were enlisted men, save the brightest if not the best, my Aunt Edna's oldest, who was I believe a captain when his plane went down off Spain. In the town park was a great bulletin board with the names of all the men in service during the war; younger kids would stop and find names of relatives, and I always had more than anyone else to count. On the playground we vied with each other in military imitations, calling each other when angry dumb Nazis or dirty Japs and trying sneaky jujitsu throws we had seen in the movies; we collected military unit patches and insignia sent home by our servicemen, and I proudly wore an Air Corps shoulder patch and Marine sergeant's stripes on my jacket. Every family with someone in service got to hang a red-bordered white flag in their front window, with a blue star for a serviceman, multiple stars for multiple sons, and a gold star for those killed. My grandmother hung a flag with stars for nine grandsons and one for my Uncle Charlie, her son-in-law; it seemed to be a record for our town—at least she got her picture in the paper, standing in front of her house with the flags in the background, and pictures of all ten of her family in uniform. Nine of ten survived the war, and when they were all home the family had a great Christmas party in a rented hall. That would have been Christmas of 1945, when I was thirteen years old.

The Christmas party was an annual tradition for a number of years. We all drew names for gifts. One year my grandmother drew my name; I was already notorious for reading, and she got me a book called *Gary Grayson's Winning Touchdown*, which I lament having lost; another Christmas the Rabbitshooter drew my name, and I got a set of little Uncle Wiggly books, also lost, but I think someone else did his shopping for him. Everyone bought Christmas trees from my Uncle Ernie, who made a small business that way; but my family got ours free as a birthday gift to my brother Roger because Aunt Freda was his baptismal godmother, and each family took that office seriously. The big event of the year, though, was the family reunion, held each summer at the picnic grounds at South Twin Lake; it ranked each year with Christmas, the Fourth of July, and the county fair. It was organized annually by a rotating committee of wives and older girl cousins; mainly it was an orgy of eating (I don't recall beer or whiskey ever), and each of the older married women had special dishes for the potluck dinner you could count on year after year—fried chicken rolled in corn flakes, potato salad with diced beet pickles, chocolate layer cake with a marshmallow center, apple pie with raisins and walnuts, eggplant casserole—so that as the dishes passed up and down the tables each dish would be recognized and acknowledged with calls of appreciation. New brides and younger women would make tentative offerings, always generously praised; girlfriends and boyfriends and those more formally affianced to the family, invited as a kind of rite of passage, ate with their sponsoring families, and nothing was expected of them except to offer themselves for inspection and discussion afterward. My grandmother, and sometimes her sister Minnie, would sit in state in lawn chairs, large, soft, bulky women, bulgy and sagging from years of childbearing and good eating. After dinner some of the men took naps on blankets in the grass and the women talked and tended babies while the older kids had to wait an hour to go in swimming so we wouldn't get cramps and drown, but my Uncle Ernie had one of the few outboard motors in town, so he took us for boat rides in gangs of six or eight, the boat riding low in the water, so that mothers could worry about us drowning an hour early. By then, a couple of the men would have gone back to town to Miller's Dairy and returned with a huge tub of ice cream packed in dry ice, and after ice cream, and the nappers had woken up, there would be entertainment, planned by the committee. Some of the older cousins would sing popular songs, and someone could tap-dance a little, and someone's boyfriend once brought an accordion, but it never appeared again so she must not have married him.

Once, though, there was a quiz show modeled on *Truth or Consequences* on the radio. One of the older cousins had found a magazine humor column in which proverbs, popular phrases, and song and movie titles had been expanded into ridiculous verbosity; if you had a Good Vocabulary, you could penetrate to the underlying meaning; if not, you could turn the page upside down and read the answers. For our entertainment, the Consequence of failure was some silly penalty, like wearing your wife's hat, or kissing your sister's husband; the prizes for Truth were candy bars and cigarettes. The game was for adults; I think I was ten years old that year as I sat with the rest of the kids and watched my uncles and aunts and grown cousins going down to defeat. I quickly caught on.

"Do not calculate the number of your juvenile poultry before the incubation has completely matured."

Uncle Ray could not translate, so he had to give up his belt and suspenders and hold his pants up, hands in pockets, for the duration of the game.

"Does the audience know?" the quizmaster mimicked the radio show. But no one answered.

"Don't count your chickens before they're hatched," I shouted. Heads swiveled toward me, and there were some laughs.

Next was my big cousin Jim, Freda's Jim, home on leave from the Marines. "Mending a flaw in fabric immediately will probably save extensive repairs at a later date."

Jim grinned in embarrassment; he was sentenced to eat a stalk of celery, the other end held in the lips of his brother's girlfriend.

"Audience?"

I already had my hand up. "A stitch in time saves nine!"

A moment of silence, then murmuring as people put their heads together. I was enjoying this, collecting candy bars.

Several other contestants went down to their defeat and my triumph. "A heated caldron under close and continuous observation as its temperature rises toward 212 degrees Fahrenheit will never achieve that ultimate temperature."

"An entire life of labor with no periods of recreation tends to make John a youth of dubious mental accomplishment."

"Unambitious skeletal remains, seated in the warmth of solar rays."

By now, the entire long table was silent. I was conscious of focused attention. One of my failed cousins was trying to pat his head and rub his stomach at the same time. The quizmaster was starting to get embarrassed. The next contestant was supposed to be Uncle Charlie, then my father.

My Aunt Caroline stood up. "I don't think we're smart enough for this game," she laughed. "I brought my Bingo cards. Anyone want to play?"

There was a smattering of applause; conversation broke out again. Caroline brought out the cards and a fruit jar of shelled corn to use as markers.

I went in swimming again. One of my older cousins pushed me off the dock and held my head under water. "Smart-ass show-off," he said. And so I was.

V

Somewhere in those years the fault line began to develop. My cousin Teddy and I separated off into different academic tracks; we traveled in different crowds, although we often walked to school together. In the eighth grade I began formal catechism to be entered as a communicant in our church. I had gone to Sunday school intermittently, as my parents had gone to church, the religious part of our extended family's lives being more a matter of form and habit than enthusiasm, and distributed unevenly throughout the various families and generations. My catechism class went easily enough; some of my close friends were in it with me, and I found the rote memorization of our creed easy and helped my friends with it as we walked to the church every Wednesday after school. We were instructed by Reverend Schalm, father of the renegade Tarzan boy, who had instructed my father twenty-some years earlier—I have the picture of his class—and who tended to confuse me with him, our names being identical, and who sometimes asked me about my church-delinquent uncles as if they were my brothers; I wanted to ask him about his Tarzan son, but I never did. I was examined in front of the congregation and took my first communion in a new suit, the point being, in the family, to admire the suits and confirmation dresses as much as the responses, except that my class was the first to wear robes at confirmation, so the finery went unobserved, to a general grumbling in the family. But I had some inkling of something deeper in that rote preparation and ritual that I did not understand, and that no one else did either, and I began to feel profoundly uncomfortable as everyone else in the congregation seemed to move comfortably on paths invisible to me. One of my emerging freedoms as I separated myself from my parents was to leave off even intermittent attendance at church, and some kind of watershed was passed when my mother, having committed the family to a weekly donation in special envelopes, and having not had the money for several months, finally insisted that I go to an evening service with a batch of overdue envelopes, finally filled with my father's bonus check, I believe. I went early, dropped the envelopes into the offering plate in the empty church, and went downtown to hang out with my friends. My Aunt Edna, my family baptismal sponsor, and hence my godmother, gave me a fine check on my confirmation and later chided me on my falling away; and on Reverend Schalm's retirement, the new, vigorous minister accosted me on the street, and I learned to watch for him as I watched for our landlord, to avoid embarrassment.

I was beginning to make distinctions between blue-collar and white-collar families, between professional lives and lives of wage labor. I was beginning to identify with the families of my mother's sisters, a lawyer's family and a teacher's family, and to suspect that somehow my mother had married beneath her possibilities into my father's family of conspicuous nonachievers. As I went up through high school, I began to skip the summer reunions for more important pursuits, though once I took two of my buddies and stayed long enough for the famous food before we went off to drink beer in a country cemetery. My senior year I made the ritual visits to each aunt and uncle to leave my framed graduation picture, which would ensure a card with congratulations and a few dollars in it and would sit on an endtable until displaced by next year's graduating cousin's picture. I graduated from high school in a ceremony full of personal honors, my cousin Teddy well back in the undistinguished middle, and my Aunts Marguerite and Caroline bought both of us new watches, as they had done for years as incentives to their nieces and nephews who stayed in high school to gradu-

ation. That summer I prepared to go away to college, and my grandmother sent word for me to come and see her; she had found some old
clothing about my size that she wanted me to have, some things that
an older cousin had left behind, and she painfully mounted the steep
stairs to a bedroom to find the box for me; but it was terrible stuff I
would not wear and I left it with the Salvation Army. Still the family
had not given up on me: my Aunt Edna paid me well for mowing her
lawn, and her husband, Uncle Leo, let me know that he had some
money saved if I ran low at college; and I even heard that the Kirsch
family, whose factory had employed my father and mother and uncles
and cousins for years, and in the shadow of which I still lived, stood
ready to back me up if my money ran out. A few years later I graduated and married at home in the Lutheran church, which had not yet
dropped me, because my bride wanted a church wedding and I was
more closely connected with a church than she was. A formal church
wedding was a step up for my family, which tended to home weddings
and civil ceremonies; my grandmother, aging badly now and moving
with difficulty, was helped to the ceremony and gave us a hand-cro-
cheted doily done in her eighty-fourth year. The reception was in a
modest style that nonetheless strained my family's social habits; my
father ended up in the boiler room talking to the building janitor, an
old friend of his, and I went away on my honeymoon and then to the
West Coast for graduate school. "Ain't you done with college *yet?*" my
Uncle Ray asked.

By this time my parents were living directly across from my grandmother and Caroline, having moved there from the abandoned county-farm dormitory where they had lived after being evicted from the
house next to the factory, where I had lived throughout high school.
My Aunt Caroline had found the house for them, and had perhaps
paid the first month's deposit. It was a great location for my father, just
a few blocks from his truck terminal, and he could park his truck on
the street in front of his mother's just as he had done twenty years
before, and stop to visit her, calling out as he always did, "Here's your
favorite son!" before he came across the street to see my mother. Aunt
Marguerite lived just down at the corner, and Freda and Ernie just a
few blocks over, so that when he slipped into his last illness, which lasted three years, he had company as he sat at home, tending my younger

brothers while my mother went to work in the toy factory. From the West Coast I kept waiting for him to recover, as he always had, and then I had to write to say that his first grandson, my first child, had died, and then my grandmother died, and then he died. Of his family, Edith and Rose had died first; then my Uncle John's heart stopped as he worked his second job pumping gas, and he did not live to see Kelly's Woods, home of naked young Tarzans, become a subdivision of that name, with grand homes he could never have lived in; and then my Uncle James's heart stopped as he sat on the toilet at the factory, and my grandmother had outlived four of her eleven children. Then my father's heart went in its special way, and then Uncle Albert's, despite his even giving up fried chicken after his first attack, and at age twenty-eight I bought a diet book by Ancel Keyes and began to exercise regularly. And cancer galloped its way through the bodies of my remaining aunts, as it had through Edith's and Rose's and my grandmother's, except that Freda preempted its progress by dying in a car accident, and Edna would succumb only to old age; but it has begun its work on the second generation of my female cousins, while the men's hearts are giving out in my generation as well, and the Lutheran church is seeing them all out as it saw them in.

V I

The younger women tried to keep up the summer family reunion after my grandmother died, but it got smaller and smaller each year. I went to the one the year I came home from the Army, introducing my wife and daughter to a remnant of the old gathering, a bare twenty people who could bother to come where before we could muster a hundred. A few of my older cousins were there, but we no longer knew each other and we talked uncomfortably. As the years have passed, my sister has come to look like my Aunt Freda, and my brother Charlie like his late namesake cousin, and I seek my own resemblance to my mother's family instead, but there is the mark on me of my Uncle Albert as a young man, and I have my grandmother's reedy voice, and nobody resembles my grandmother more than my oldest daughter, she of the many children. Of my grandmother's children, only my Uncle Ray remains, feeble with age and dim-sighted with cataracts and glaucoma, and when I ask him about the old days he says, "I was the baby. Most everything happened before I was born." My brother James looks like my father as a young man; he lives alone in my mother's house, while across the street strangers live in the house of my grandmother, and there are no aunts and uncles to walk to and visit. Asphalt now covers the driveway of my grandmother's house, even over the cement where once my footprints were marked and initialed, and when I looked and did not find them I felt a lightness in my body, an evanescence, as though I had just learned I had never been born. I longed to go to the garage to see if my Aunt Marguerite's collection of legs was still there, and I wondered if the doctrine of the resurrection of the body, complete and incorruptible on Judgment Day, had given special consolation to her for a foot buried in a tin box, or to my Uncle Dingy for the fingers that had once held a beer bottle in a man's full-fingered grasp. And I wonder now if for any of that family heaven could have meant any greater joy than another reunion, an elect one hundred gathered at picnic tables on a summer Sunday, eating and drinking and laughing through a mammoth potluck dinner at once perfect and never ending.

Two Fingers

M Y FATHER DIED UNDER the surgeon's knife
on the morning of June 12, 1957, one day short of his
forty-seventh birthday. I was then twenty-five years old.
He had been obviously and continuously ill for three
years, and in that time we had finally come to understand the occasional frightening spells of weakness that
would clamp down on him in the years of his manhood.
Sometime as a child he had contracted rheumatic fever;
it had damaged the mitral valve of his heart, constricting
the flow of blood and overburdening the heart muscle.
After years of abuse, the heart was failing.

"Mitral stenosis," the doctor told us after the tests,
circling two fingers of one hand with the thumb and fore-
finger of the other. "That valve ought to open two fingers wide, and it's about the size of a pencil."

I came home on leave from the Army the day before
the operation was scheduled. We met that night in the
hospital waiting room, and a nurse brought my father
down in a wheelchair; he looked apologetic and embarrassed. He held my infant daughter in his lap for a while.
We talked randomly until the nurse took him away
again. He managed a smile and a wave as the elevator
doors closed.

He had taken the bus to the hospital that morning,
leaving my brothers with my aunt while my mother

worked. The hospital was across the street from a park, where he sat on a bench for a while. Then he walked over to a tavern on the corner for a forbidden beer and ham-and-cheese sandwich. At noon he checked himself in and waited for nightfall and the gathering of his family.

"The doctor says he has a fifty-fifty chance," my mother said.

Heart surgery was a primitive craft in those days, not yet made familiar by cheerful survivors and television documentaries. I could imagine only a knife slicing into a jumping muscle. I remember thinking that fifty-fifty odds was a hero's bet, John Wayne flipping a coin. My mother and my sister and I sat in a small waiting room high up in the hospital. From the window I could look down on the little park and the tavern with a neon Schlitz sign. Two men stood at the door talking. In the park the benches were empty in the sunshine, but a mother was pushing a child in a swing.

In the middle of the morning a nurse came into the room and spoke to us. "Mr. Holtz is not doing so well," she said. "You had better prepare yourselves for the worst."

We all stood up. My mother reached for my hand. A few minutes later two doctors came in, still in their operating gowns. The surgeon, a tall, bony man, his face damp with sweat, gave us the news.

"We found a blood clot. It must have been there for years. Just as we opened up the heart, it slipped away." He held his hand up, two long fingers pressed against his thumb. "I almost had it. I had it right in my fingertips, and it slipped away. It went right to his brain. I'm very sorry."

They left us alone. There were no tears, not even from my mother; for all of us, that saving flux of grief had leached away in years of intermittent alarms, leaving simply a grief already irreducible as a stone. "I've been ready for this for years," she said quietly. And so had we all. My father had been dying for almost as long as I had known him.

The nurse brought us my father's clothes in a brown paper grocery bag. I recognized his good blue suit, his polished shoes. She was carrying his derby hat, which would fit in the bag only awkwardly. "I didn't want to crush it," she whispered. I carried the bag in one hand and the derby hat in the other as we went down in the elevator. My mother went in my sister's car. I put the bag and the hat on the seat of my car beside me, the hat on top of the bag so it would not fall off on the floor. I had worn it sometimes as a child, the brim down around my ears. I reached home ahead of my sister and my mother. I walked into the house with the bag and the hat.

My aunt was dozing in a chair while my brothers watched television. I put the bag and the hat down on the dining room table and began to wonder how I could explain that this was all that was left of my father.

The first thing that I can remember my father doing when we moved to the little house in the country was to make me a swing. I was six that year, 1938, and my father was twenty-eight; and my continuous memory does not go back much further. I recall that when I was four we lived in an apartment in Cleveland, where he had a job driving truck; then we came back to Michigan to live in my grandmother's house briefly until we moved for a year into another apartment while my father went to work in a factory. He had a car then that I now know was a Ford Model A, and he had that car when we moved to a small bungalow for the year that I spent in kindergarten. Then he did not have the car, the man with the hook had taken it away, he said; and we lived for a summer in one front room of my uncle's house, sharing a dinner table and everything else with my aunt and uncle and their five children. Then my father had a car again, and in the fall of 1938 we moved to the little house in the country. It was a terrible house, a tumbledown ruin with a windmill for water and an outhouse for comfort, and my mother could never speak of it without pain; but in the three years we lived there I came fully from infancy into the world. Wordsworth was right: at a certain age the places of our world luminesce with a special significance. That house and its environs haunt my thoughts like no other place I have ever lived. It is the permanent home of my imagination.

It was called the old Mahle place. Ruth Mahle had left it when she married Frank Harker and moved to a larger and more modern house just up the road, from which the Harkers now managed the substantial farm that Ruth had brought to her marriage. Just down the road in the other direction, a place I passed as I walked to school, was the collapsed ruin of an earlier home known as the old Mahle homestead. This sequence of homes was my first history and sociology lesson: that there were people whose lives were continuous in place and property, and there were people like us, whose lives were not. The Harkers were our landlords, decent and kindly people who treated us well; the place we lived in still had large barns that were part of the farming operations, and several small outbuildings that we were free to use. All were in better shape than the house. The survivors of old perennial flower beds bloomed around the house—irises and lilies of the valley and some poppies and hollyhocks, all of them untended for years and untended by us as well—and a tangled and abandoned orchard gave us a small yield of wormy apples. A horseshoe drive curved around the back door and returned to the road, and within the horseshoe the front yard was graced with large pine trees that must have been planted a century before. These trees housed the resident spirits of the place, I am sure. I played beneath them as among the feet of giants, who overhead held high converse in the fitful breeze of summer. Under one of these pine trees, right next to the road, my father and I stood and considered the swing.

He had salvaged the end of a board from somewhere and some old hay ropes from a barn; the day before I had watched as he drilled holes in the board with an auger. The limb he had his eye on must have been thirty feet up. He had tried to throw a knotted end of a rope up and over but had failed, and we put things away for that day. But now he had brought from town a small bow-and-arrow set, a child's toy stapled in a piece of cardboard, and a ball of kite string. He tied the string to one of the arrows, and with a few tries he shot it over the limb. With the string he pulled the ropes up and over, and then snugged them up with slipknots. He cut the free ends to length, slipped them through the holes in the board, and knotted them. I had a swing and a bow-and-arrow set.

The arc to that swing was tremendous, putting to shame any playground swing. I could stand on the seat holding the ropes and pump myself into great, looping rises and falls, soaring with the rhythmic creaking of ropes into the privileged atmosphere of the giant trees and out again. At the end of each arc I would be almost parallel to the ground; momentum all but overcame gravity and the board loosened beneath my feet. At the full height of the forward swing I could just see over the crest of the hill to where the descending crossroad from our corner came into view again. This was the road my father took to town each day at four, to work the afternoon shift. As he left, I would begin pumping in the swing, and for a few moments I could catch glimpses of his car as it curved along the road to town—one glimpse at the top of my arc, another seconds later, sometimes maybe a third. My body strained to fly; the temptation was to let go and fly; inevitably I did, just once. I discovered the precedence of gravity over momentum, the ineluctable weight of the body, and, scraped and bleeding, an intimation of my own mortality in the hot afternoon dust of the road.

The bow-and-arrow set was less dangerous. The arrows were tipped with suction cups; they were supposed to stick to a target on the back of the cardboard they were mounted on, but they did not. One rainy afternoon my father showed me how they would stick to a window-pane if the suction cups were wet with spit. We spent the afternoon shooting the flies that buzzed against the window glass while my mother complained mildly about the mess.

The car that my father had now was a 1929 Chevrolet. It had a cracked radiator, which meant that it had to be filled with water daily. In the warm weather of summer and fall this was no problem, but in the winter it cost too much to keep it filled with alcohol and it would freeze if left to stand with water in it. So my father would drain the radiator and refill it twice a day, at home and at work. In very cold weather he would just leave the car running with a brick on the accelerator, refilling it more often. After one cold snap, when he had forgotten to leave it running, the gas line was frozen. My father heated it with his blowtorch. I was frightened when a small fire started flaring from the tubing under the hood, but my father merely shoveled snow on the flame until it went out.

On Saturday nights we would go to town, my parents to shop for groceries and I to go to the library for books. Sometimes on the way home a rabbit would leap along the road in front of us, dodging the oncoming headlights, and my father would swerve and speed up to try to hit it. And sometimes as we turned into the drive of our house a rabbit would start, and we would pursue it through the yard, circling wildly around the pine trees and cutting between the outbuildings. I thought this was great, whooping fun, but my mother was usually holding fast to the door handle and murmuring, "Oh, my God, Bill, stop!" I don't recall that we ever got a rabbit this way; but my father claimed to have done it at least once and was still trying. I do know that from time to time he would come home with a chicken that "got in the way," as he said; there were several farms between home and town where chickens ranged freely up and down the road. Jokes about eating roadkill are jokes from more prosperous times; we ate the chickens, as we ate the rabbits and squirrels he did get with his shotgun. We also ate snapping turtles that he picked up where the road curved around a lake, although these came home alive in a burlap bag in the back seat.

It must have been the following spring that the first door fell off the car. The winter roads were frozen into washboard ruts; the car rattled in an irregular rhythm over the whole four miles twice a day, and the doors loosened and got harder to close. Halfway to town was a railroad-grade crossing, a steep rise and fall in the road. It was just possible to take the crossing fast enough to get a thrill in the pit of the stomach. Probably I had learned this because my father had done it once deliberately. Each time we approached the crossing I shouted for my father to speed up; my mother would say please don't and my father would laugh and tromp the accelerator and we would leap and drop over the crossing. I suspect we were airborne a couple of times; certainly we were the time we hit the road with a lurch that tore the wheel from my father's hands momentarily. The door on my mother's side flew open and hung by one hinge. We came home very slowly.

Nineteen-twenty-nine was the last year Fischer Body made wooden doorposts for the Chevrolet chassis they supplied to General Motors, my father explained to me. He managed to reattach the door temporarily, but the car was doomed. Hinge screws would not hold in the rotted wooden doorposts, and by summer all four doors were gone. The canvas roof began to leak through onto the seats, and one day a strong wind peeled a corner of the roof back into a flapping rag. My father bought another car he thought he could repair if he could find a carburetor for it; meantime, the Chevrolet was air-conditioned, he said, just right for summer driving. He cut the remaining body off just above the seats, making it into a roadster. The seats by now were moldering sponges, so he took them out, replacing the back seat with an old wagon bench and the front seat with two kitchen chairs screwed to the floorboards. My mother rode in silent terror, but I thought it was a purely wonderful car, and it began a wonderful, terrible summer.

My father did not have to be at work until late afternoon, and in the heat of the summer he would take us all to the swimming beach at Grey Lake. From midmorning until well past noon my sister and I could swim; there were usually a few other families there on the same schedule; my mother would read a magazine and lay out a picnic lunch while my father talked and laughed with other men from the factory who worked the same shift. Then we would speed home just in time for him to make the return trip to work. My father had lost the radiator cap after one of the many refillings and had replaced it with a tin can; on the Fourth of July some practical joker in the paint shop at the factory had painted it red, white, and blue and had done the same to the wheels, as well as to my father's lunch pail. The muffler was gone and the engine roared like a tractor; the hot exhaust flared against the wooden floorboards and one day set them and our picnic basket on fire beneath my mother's feet; in a flurry of charred boards and smoldering towels and the burnt remains of sandwiches my father beat out the flames with wet bathing suits and, wrapping his hands in towels, broke off the exhaust pipe at the manifold. Day after day we roared along the country roads. The wind blew our hair dry, I made a banner of my towel, and everyone we passed would smile and wave. One day we racketed through a white cloud of chickens down the road from a farmhouse. My father leaned to his left and made a quick grab, and suddenly a flopping Leghorn was in the car with us; a twist of the wrist and its neck was broken and it lay beneath my feet in the back seat. No one had a car like ours. My mother hoped the other car would be running by winter.

Despite such bright days we were living through dark times. My parents had married in the trough of the Depression and had brought two children into the world on an intermittent income barely enough for themselves. My father never found the toehold that would let him take a step ahead; in fact, I believe that he was fatally incapable of that kind of foresight. For several years early in their marriage they had had to live apart, my mother and my sister and I with her parents while my father sent what money he could when he could find work. As I retrace their lives it is clear that only the nominal rent for our decaying farmhouse made it possible for them to stay together now. My mother was pregnant again, I learned from my schoolmates who heard it from their parents; I did not understand quite what this meant, but as my parents talked I could feel that particular worry compound with the general worry about money.

One day that summer they gave me a quarter to pay for two ten-cent circus tickets for me and my sister; they waited outside while we went to the show. And I lost the nickel in change! Down in the grass beneath the bleachers I searched while the ringmaster whipped the ponies around, and I could not find it. I missed most of the show. The dismay in my mother's face shames me yet today, and I have never been able to enjoy a circus since. My bow-and-arrow set cost fifty cents, and my father's willingness to spend so impulsively was a symptom of his larger failure to thrive. The winter just past was brutal, from my mother's accounts; there was only the kitchen range for heat; snow crept in under the doors. My parents and sister slept in the room next to the kitchen; I slept in a bedroom with a kerosene heater, beneath my father's dress overcoat in lieu of an extra blanket. I must have been cold regularly, but I do not remember it. Spring and summer must have come as some kind of primitive, elemental relief, so that in that summer of 1939 we were all happier than we had any right to be.

Without its muffler my father's car roared so joyously that I usually awoke when he came home past midnight. Sometimes I would go out and sit with my parents in the kitchen, or just lie in my bed and listen to them talk. They talked of moving but could not find the money. They talked of my grandmother coming in the fall to help with the baby. They talked of my father's trouble finding a carburetor for the new car. They talked of raising chickens: "Our own eggs and fried chicken every Sunday." They talked one night of my father's sudden illness. "I couldn't drive," he said. "I had to pull over and put my head out the window. I thought I was going to pass out. I was sweating like a thresher." Then later: "Doc Miller thinks it's something wrong with my heart. He says I have an enlarged heart, he says it's been working too hard." Worry was my mother's business, and as I grew into a realization of our tenuous hold on life I began to share it with her. My father had no talent for it. His talent was for fun and laughter and the inspired expedient that put off each day's threat of chaos until tomorrow.

Saturdays and Sundays he did not have to work; I remember mainly that he puttered to keep the Chevy running or to get the other car to run at all before winter came on again. On Saturday nights we would listen to the National Barn Dance with Lulubelle and Scotty and Minnie Pearl and the Blue-Eyed Boy; my father would sing in a husky, pleasant tenor, and I would sing with him:

> Come and sit by my side if you love me,
> Do not hasten to bid me adieu . . .

On Sunday afternoon he would sit in the kitchen while my mother fixed dinner, a bottle of whiskey and a shot glass on the table. The radio programs were different and so were the songs: "Red Sails in the Sunset" (Red Who? my father would ask, laughing at me); "I Don't Want to Set the World on Fire"; "Oh, Mama! Get That Man for Me"; "I Have a Rancho Grande." All of these I can still sing. By dinnertime he was in glowing good spirits; he would pull my mother down on his lap and hug her; she, embarrassed in front of me, would pull away. Wayne King the Waltz King would play as we ate, and chaos was forestalled for another day.

Although this bids fair to be a story about cars, chickens and guns and dogs seem all mixed up in that summer of 1939. The chickens came first, early in the spring, dozens of peeping balls of fluff in cardboard boxes that we kept warm behind the stove. One of the old outbuildings was a chicken house, and my father strung some chicken-wire fencing to make a small run for them. He had got Leghorns, the wildest and most athletic of domestic birds, rather than the more tractable Plymouth Rocks or Rhode Island Reds. One of my earliest memories of guns is of the startling *ka-blam!* that jerked me from my sleep early one summer morning. I ran downstairs to find my father in the yard in his underwear with his double-barrel twelve-gauge on his arm. "Damn woodpecker!" he said, holding up a bloody rag of feathers in one hand. He had been trying to finish out his night's sleep; the woodpecker had found something in the rotting wall of the house and had hammered after it too persistently, until my father blasted the hungry bird into woodpecker heaven with a load of number-six bird shot. A bright scar of fresh wood marked the place on the side of the house for as long as we lived there.

I suppose guns figured regularly in our lives because the gully at the end of one of the fields behind our house was a natural target range for sighting-in deer rifles. My father did not have a deer rifle, but my uncles did, and in our first fall there and in the next as well they brought their rifles out for practice, and the gully rang with gunfire and I collected the empty cartridge casings around the men's feet and became adept at distinguishing my Uncle Dingy's .30/06 and my Uncle Dewey's .303 and my Uncle Bing's booming .45/70 from the mere .30/30 of my Uncle Ray and the .35 caliber of my Uncle Roy. They shot at targets drawn on cardboard boxes and at cans and bottles and old planks. My father hoped to go deer hunting with them; he had bought some rifled deer slugs for his shotgun. They fired into an old stump and then dug out the bullets to compare the mushrooming of the hollow-points and the copperjackets and my father's slugs. Then there would be beer drinking in the kitchen, and someone would bring out a bottle, and there would be talk of hunts past and hunts planned and learned discussion of flat trajectories and muzzle velocities and brush busters, and I would wonder how my Uncle Dingy, who had lost the two middle fingers of one hand, could have such a perfect three-pronged claw for holding a beer bottle. My father never did go deer hunting, but he often went for squirrels on fall weekends and for rabbits in the winter, and we would eat small fried pieces of meat and pick the lead pellets out with our forks.

His shotgun had been his father's, and I never learned how it came to be his, since he was one of the youngest of the sons. It was a J. C. Stevens, a common make, and in later years one trigger spring was broken when I sometimes used it. The other guns that belong in this story are my father's two pistols, one a .25 caliber automatic and the other a .22 revolver. He had taken them as security on a twenty-dollar loan to Ted Foster, and when my mother would remind him of the loan he would say, "That's the only time Ted Foster ever had twenty dollars all together, and he'll never have it again." He had carried the tiny, palm-sized .25 caliber in his boot as protection when he was driving truck; the .22 revolver turned out to have a broken firing pin, and when he could not fix it he filed off the pin and gave the disabled gun to me as a toy. "You can have it till Ted Foster pays up, and I don't think you have to worry." From an old boot top he cut out a leather holster for me and had it stitched together at the shoe-repair shop. Tom Mix was my cowboy hero; I listened to his radio show each week and took his pledge to be a straight shooter and eat Ralston cereal, and I loaded the cylinder of my revolver with spent .22 casings and practiced my quick draw against the day Ted Foster might try to reclaim his pawn. No kid I knew had a gun like mine.

My father ate early, before he went to work; often my mother, my sister, and I would eat a separate supper later. One evening as we were eating, a man came across the fields in back of our house and made his way to the kitchen door. He was ragged and dirty, older than my father, with shaggy gray hair and a short beard. A white film covered one eye, and he carried a blanket roll and a stick. The Depression had turned thousands like him out on the roads in those years, but this was our tramp in our family history and the reason we got Pal and then Spot and then Dick. Where he had come from, why across the fields rather than along the road, we never knew. He wanted a meal. My mother prepared a plate of beans and eggs for him and handed it out the door; he sat on our back step and ate. My mother latched the screen door and then closed the inner door, even though the air was stifling hot.

She stood with her back against the door and her finger across her lips, signaling my sister and me to be quiet. We sat silent for long minutes; we could hear the scrape of the knife and fork on the plate outside. Then his voice, hoarse and pleading. "Ma'am, I need a place to sleep tonight. Maybe I could sleep in your barn?"

My mother was shaking her head quietly at us, finger still on her lips. Moments of silence.

"Ma'am, I'm plumb wore out walking. I need a rest. Maybe I could sleep in that old Pontiac you got in the shed? I'll be gone in the morning."

He rattled the screen door. We sat in paralyzed silence. We heard slow steps drag across the porch, and then he was standing at the window, hands cupped to his face, peering in at us, trying to see with his one eye into the gloom of the kitchen. My mother was not in his view, but my sister and I were. Whether he could see us I don't know; a moment later he was gone. From the front room we could see him walking down the horseshoe drive; at the road he turned neither right nor left but went on across the field into the twilight and out of our lives.

My father said, "You know, my little automatic is in the bureau drawer. Or all you'd have to do is just point the shotgun at him. He'd clear out fast."

"Oh, I could never do that," my mother said. In my mind's eye I could see myself quick-drawing on the tramp as he came through our kitchen door. *Reach for the sky, hombre!* His wretched, hopeless face hangs in my mind to this day.

"We better get a dog," my father said.

A few days later he came home with Pal. I'm sure he didn't buy him; I think Ted Foster was in the line of transmittal somewhere, a natural agent for the end-of-the-line, useless items of the world. I suspect no one had ever wanted Pal for more than two days; whoever had had him last even sent along a small, rickety doghouse. Pal was a pure delinquent, black and tan with signs of collie and spaniel in his makeup. He was obsequiously friendly, a whining, tail-thumping, belly-crawling, hand-licking craven of a mongrel. I had not heard of a hangdog expression then, but when I did I'm sure Pal was the image. "Ted says he'll bark like hell if anybody comes to the door."

Pal was a barker. He stood in the kitchen at the screen door and barked incessantly whether anyone was there or not. Finally my father opened the door and Pal was away like a shot, across the fields and out of sight in moments. "We've fed him once; he'll be back," my father said.

Pal was back the next afternoon, crouching at the door and licking his hip. My father found blood and some shotgun pellets embedded in his skin. He tied Pal to the porch and rubbed the wound with kerosene. A little later Frank Harker came down to talk to us. "Jess Taylor had a dog running his cows yesterday. Says he shot at it. Looks like it might be this fella here."

My father nodded his agreement. "Okay. We'll have to keep him tied up, I guess."

Pal was tied to his doghouse near the back step, where he barked for hours on end. After a few days my father moved him out near the chicken house. All that would stop him would be to pet him while he cowered around your ankles. But his character was not yet fully revealed.

Our chickens were reaching full size now; we were getting a few eggs and eating a few fryers. Leghorns are notorious fliers, though, and they were more often outside the pen than in. My father clipped the wings of some of them, but a few were always loose. One morning we came out to find Pal's area strewn with bloody feathers and Pal tossing a limp carcass around. My father beat him soundly with the dead chicken. "Maybe that'll teach him," he said.

It became clear that Pal could be a barking nuisance or a quiet killer. When a chicken was near, he fell silent and lay quietly as the bird wandered closer and closer, finally to within the length of his chain. Then with a quick lunge he had his quarry by the neck, shaking it furiously. Beatings did no good. Pal was incorrigible. At last one day my father took down his shotgun and a shovel and put Pal on a rope; they headed across the field toward the gully. My mother put her hands over my ears, but I heard the blast just the same.

Our next dog was Spot, more or less borrowed from my Uncle John, whose wife wanted to be rid of the dog. Spot was vaguely beagle-ish; he did not bark or chase cows or kill chickens. He did nothing but sit in the sun and gaze hopefully at the back door; he would not even get up unless we came with a plate of food in hand. In a few weeks my uncle came back for him, having won his wife over to Spot's return.

We were dogless for a while after Spot, and I would sneak sometimes to handle my father's .25 caliber automatic in the bureau drawer. It was smaller than my broken pistol; nickel plated and with ivory grips, it just fit my hand; I was sure I could use it if the tramp returned. The shotgun over the door was obviously more than I could handle. But then my father came home with Dick, a large brown-and-white dog sitting confident as a policeman in the back seat of the '29 Chevy.

Dick was a powerful dog, as large as a boxer, although when I later saw a picture of a mastiff it looked familiar. Once he was established with us, he was a good watchdog, a growler rather than a barker when anyone came around. But we had to keep him chained, because he would attack. He took Frank Harker's pants leg off one Sunday afternoon when Frank got within range of his chain. Dick had no taste for chickens, though, and my sister and I played with him without fear; and we lived without fear of wandering tramps. But Dick was too big for the little doghouse he inherited from the late Pal, and my father went to work to build a new one.

I saw my father happy in many ways—he was almost always happy; I saw him happy in singing and happy in drink and good company and happy in his fondness for my mother; but if he was characteristically happy in work it was in turning his hand to craft a small marvel out of next to nothing. He came home one day with a stack of fine, bright boards he had salvaged from packing crates at the factory. I held boards while he sawed; he whistled and sang and measured and did fractions on the backs of boards. At the end of the day a majestic house stood ready for Dick. Sturdy and square, it had a gable roof that stood as tall as my head. In one corner was a door hole with a flap of carpet over it to keep out drafts; in the other wall was a small glass window "so's he can see who's coming." The sides and roof were covered in tar paper against the weather. Inside it was piney smelling and bright; I could crawl in with Dick and so could my sister, and it became instantly a playhouse, cozy, safe, and defensible—I would sit with my back to the wall, my .22 pistol in hand, snapping the pinless hammer on empty cartridge casings, ready for whatever came. We peered out the window at my worried mother, who feared Dick's fleas, and Dick bore our company patiently. Dick's house was better than ours, I now see clearly; once, later, as these things were dawning on me, I asked my father if he could build a whole house. "Easy," he said. "If I could salvage enough lumber, and had somewhere to put it."

And so as the glorious summer of 1939 wore down into fall I walked uncomprehending among terrors I sensed but could not name. My mother was frightened of nights alone in an isolated farmhouse. A baby was due in the hard winter months. We had half a car that would run and a whole car that would not. My father's heart—I imagined it enlarging in his chest like a malignant valentine—murmured a quiet prophecy. Meanwhile, our flock of white Leghorn chickens had declined to a few wild and hardy survivors: some we had eaten, some had been eaten by predators, some had simply vanished; the chicken yard stood empty while the remaining band scavenged in the yard by day, and we took to scattering feed for them just here and there. They laid their eggs in hidden nests and roosted in the trees by night. Chief among them were the two roosters, Archibald and Percy my father had named them. Archibald was a broad-shouldered, big-chested bruiser, slow and deliberate in his movements. Percy was lighter, rangier and quicker. Somehow they had divided the province between them; I never saw a fight. But the day had passed when a chicken dinner was simply a matter of grabbing a docile bird and carrying it to the chopping block; these birds were skittish and unapproachable. My father showed me how to bait them in with a kernel of corn threaded onto a string. Once the bird had swallowed the corn down into its crop, it could be led like a pet to the slaughter. I discovered for myself that a captured chicken could be put into a paper grocery bag and swung vigorously around my head, producing a bird so dizzy it would stagger drunkenly in circles. A number of late surviving hens went thus to a mercifully vertiginous death, until only Archibald and Percy walked our yard by day and crowed our sun up each morning.

As our '29 Chevy shed its parts week by week through that summer, my father worked on the other car that would see us through the winter. This was a 1931 Pontiac, a sturdy car that would be with us many years. It had a good engine, my father said, except for one scored cylinder that drank oil and fouled the spark plug, but he thought he could solve that with a hotter plug. Its roof had begun to leak and it needed a carburetor, so he had gotten it for eighteen dollars and seventy-five cents: twenty dollars had been written in soap on the windshield when he brought it home. He kept it in one of the sheds while he worked on the roof and tried to rebuild the carburetor.

On Saturdays he and Ted Foster would sometimes search through the junkyards around the county for parts. My mother was always nervous when Ted Foster came by; usually it meant that my father was going someplace and would return tipsy. Ted Foster was a handsome man with quick, smiling features and a ready tongue. He worked at a gas station; he sometimes gave me nickels from the bright, clicking coin changer he wore on his belt. When he came to visit he would bring a few beers for himself and my father and a candy bar or chewing gum for me; often he would stay for dinner, to my mother's distress. I understood that he owed my father more than the twenty dollars secured by his two guns. He it was who found the roof for the '31 Pontiac. I think it was the day that the '29 Chevy lost its remaining headlight—the first having fallen off unnoticed along the road one day.

Late summer was on the verge of fall; the walnut trees around the house were beginning to yellow and were dropping nuts at a profligate rate, and my father had devised a quick and easy way of hulling them. He had built a small V-shaped trough of boards and jacked up the rear end of the Chevy so that both wheels were off the ground and one tire was just inside the trough. With the engine running and the transmission in gear, the tire spun rapidly in the trough; my father tossed walnuts into the trough in front of the tire one by one, and they shot out the other end like bullets, without their hulls. I ran through the yard beneath the pines, picking up the hulled nuts in a peach basket. Ted Foster had arrived just as the hulling started. Laughing, he began pitching walnuts in faster and faster until they were flying across the yard at me like projectiles from a Gatling gun. Then he started feeding in two and three at a time. Something caught, jammed under the tire, the car lurched off its jack and started its way across the yard. My father and Ted Foster ran after it, laughing and swearing. It stopped against the side of the shed, its remaining headlight smashed. My father was suddenly sober. "Dammit, Ted! I'm gonna have to come home without lights tonight."

But Ted's news was that he had discovered a large piece of sheet metal blown off a billboard over near White Pigeon. "Just waiting to be picked up, Bill. It would make a dandy roof for your Pontiac." I went with them to salvage it the next day. Ted had borrowed a trailer, and once we had loaded it I was seated on top of the rattling piece of sheet metal to keep it from slipping off on the journey home. It had been part of an advertisement for Camel cigarettes; the ubiquitous assertion, "I'd walk a mile for a Camel," survived only in its last word, and the camel itself remained only in its haunches and tail. After traveling in our open-air Chevy, this trip did not seem unusual; my father and Ted Foster sat in the kitchen chairs in front and glanced back from time to time to check their load. They stopped at Klinger Lake Tavern for a few beers; I sat drinking Orange Crush while my father laughingly explained to some gathered friends what he would do with the camel's rump in the trailer.

For the next several days my father worked on his new roof. He laboriously cut the sheet metal down to size with his tin snips. From the factory he brought home a small electric drill in his lunch box; it was borrowed, he said, and maybe it was, for I do not recall seeing it after that project. He drilled holes through the new roof into the metal of the passenger compartment and fastened it down tight with dozens of screws. Then he heated up his blowtorch and soldering iron and soldered the joint, a twenty-foot seam around the perimeter of the roof. From inside the car I could look up at the camel's rump and tail; most of the lettering had been trimmed away. "Now that's the way it should have been built in the first place," my father said when he was finished. Ted Foster called the car the camel-ass Pontiac.

But it still would run only feebly. Nights were getting cold, and my father came home at night, without headlights, in his jacket. We had a September frost; the maples and elms began to turn; I heard more talk of the imminent arrival of my grandmother, coming from northern Michigan to help my mother with the baby. "She can't ride in that car," my mother said firmly. I remember the excitement in my father's voice when finally he solved the carburetor problem. Was it an updraft or a downdraft carburetor that the Pontiac needed? I knew once, with the certainty that my father knew it. But he had found a carburetor from an old Plymouth that could be made to work. He laughed and hugged my mother as he explained: "The holes for the mounting bolts lined up perfect once I turned it upside down. She runs like a top now." The only problem was that the air cleaner would not fit; to the end of its days the '31 Pontiac ran with a characteristic wheeze, sucking its air impure and unfiltered into its engrafted Plymouth carburetor.

Was it because of my grandmother's imminent arrival that we needed one last chicken dinner, and that Archibald and Percy would be called upon for the final sacrifice? Things rush all together here in my memories; certain it was that she was not there for their executions, and that she arrived shortly after. I remember that we picked her up at the bus station, and I remember her pointing with amazement to the partial camel above our heads as she sat in the back seat between my sister and me, talking unintelligibly in Finnish. My mother was turned, talking to her in reply, and both were laughing. "She says, if you had paid more, could you have gotten the other end?" my mother said to my father.

My father was laughing, too. "Tell her what Ted Foster calls our car."

"I don't know the words for that," my mother said.

But this was after the end of Archibald and Percy, for my grandmother was not there on that day, although she might have arrived the day after. In my memories, her wise and merry face belongs to the time after. She had come to take care of children, and I now believe she understood that my sister and I were not her only care.

As I remember, my father was nursing a toothache that afternoon, which he sometimes did with the only medicine I ever saw him take, a bottle of whiskey; instead of swallowing the whiskey directly, he held it in his mouth over the affected tooth. I never saw him spit any out though, and he was singing with the radio from time to time as usual. Then he and I were stalking Archibald and Percy through the yard and around the outbuildings. Time after time we would converge on one of the wary birds only to see it fly over a fence or scuttle under a bush. My father was sweating and swearing.

I offered to bait them with corn and a string.

"No, that would take forever," he said. "I want to clean 'em both today before I go to work. I'm gonna hunt 'em like pheasants."

We returned to the house for his shotgun. He had just two cartridges. "One for each bird," he said. "Easy."

I walked behind him as we pursued Archibald, the larger target. The nervous bird ducked and hid and flew, an elusive quarry. For a moment it perched on the top rail of the orchard fence and my father fired. But just at that instant the bird launched himself and flew.

"Damn!" my father shouted, even as he turned and shot Archibald out of the air with the second barrel, a clean kill.

We carried Archibald's bloody carcass back to the house and hung it by the feet from the clothesline. My father went into the house and came out with his .25 caliber automatic and a box of cartridges. "Plenty of bullets," my father said. "I can just plink old Percy in the head and save the meat." I strapped on my .22 and followed him back into the yard.

Percy was strutting about unconcerned. My father braced his hand against the side of the outhouse and squeezed off a couple of rounds at Percy's head. The bird ducked nervously, then took off running around to the front of the house. He scuttled beneath the spirea bushes; my father knelt and took aim again at a figure we could barely see. At the crack of the shot, Percy squawked and flew straight up out of the spirea; he hit the ground running, and as he dashed by me I could see blood flowing from his comb. He flew onto a low limb of a pine tree, then off again, and ran toward the orchard. We both ran after him. "Head him off!" my father shouted. "Get him back into the clear."

We pursued Percy through the orchard. My father was firing at every chance now, reloading several times. I think he had given up trying for a head shot. We worked the bird back into the clear area around the outbuildings. I was trying to herd him toward my father when my mother caught me by the collar and dragged me into the house. "Get under the bed!" she said, pushing me to my knees. My sister was already under the bed. Outside, my father was still firing.

The shooting stopped for a while and I could hear my mother and father arguing in the yard. My mother said one chicken would be enough; my father said no wild Leghorn rooster was going to get the best of him. My mother came back into the house and sat in the rocking chair beside the bed. The firing commenced again, and she would not let me come out. Things were quiet for a while; then there were two quick shots just outside the window, a muffled squawking, my father swearing. He came into the house and put the gun down.

"The damn bird flew up onto the chimney. I popped him; it was an easy shot. But he's fallen down the chimney flue."

"Oh Lord, Bill, just leave him there."

"Can't. He'll smell to high heaven in a day or so, and we'll have to use the stove. Besides, I think he's still alive. Listen!"

My sister and I were out from under the bed now, and in the quiet moment we could hear Percy's faint croaking in the chimney wall. "I'll have to take the kitchen stovepipe down and try to pull him out."

We all gathered in the kitchen. My father disconnected the stovepipe at an elbow and began to work the end of the pipe out of the chimney wall. It came free with a little plaster and a trickle of soot. Then out of the dark hole in the wall the wounded Percy exploded into the room in a cloud of feathers, blood, and soot.

We were all in it now, my father and mother and my sister and I. "Keep him in the kitchen!" my father shouted as the bird rocketed from wall to wall. Percy had been hit in the neck; he was bleeding hard, but he was far from dead. The skirmish lasted only moments before my father stunned the bird with a broom and then quickly twisted its neck. He stood holding the bird, smeared with blood and soot. "Old Percy, he was a real fighter!" he laughed. We all laughed, even my mother.

He gave the bird to me. "Take him out and hang him up with the other. I'll be out to clean 'em soon as we can heat some water." He was putting the stovepipe back into the wall. My mother was beginning to sweep.

But when I came back in, the stovepipe was on the floor and my father was sitting slumped at the kitchen table, his head in his hands. His eyes were closed, his face was twisted, and he was breathing hard. My mother had her arms around him.

"You and your sister go outside and play," she said to me. "You keep an eye on her. Your father's not feeling well. He's going to go rest on the bed for a few minutes."

I wandered in the yard awhile, then crawled into Dick's great dog-house. My sister followed me, as did Dick, and we three lay in a doggy, commiserating tangle while some desperate drama played itself out in the kitchen. The world had changed; Death had reached in and tweaked my father, just a pinch with two fingers, and Dick and my disabled gun could not protect us. I watched the kitchen door through the little window. Smoke began to come from the chimney. In time, my mother came out to get us and bring us back into the kitchen. She had heated some water and was cleaning the chickens. My father was washing at the kitchen sink. We all ate with him, a very quiet meal.

I must have been in my swing again when he left for work. Do I remember it right, he is driving the open-air '29 Chevy again? The refurbished Pontiac did not displace that car at once; he drove it into the woods to haul firewood, I know, and in time its axle and rear wheels would become a trailer, and its engine would power a buzz saw to cut firewood: even severed driveshaft from differential that car would not die. But that was later; now, as I wait in my swing, here he comes, around the horseshoe drive, sitting in the kitchen chair, his red-white-and-blue lunch box at his feet, the red-white-and-blue wheels a pinwheel blur, the exhaust roaring straight from the manifold, roofless and doorless and headlightless he turns at the corner and drops out of sight below the hill on the road to town. I am standing in the swing now, pumping hard, in greater and greater arcs, and at the peak of the arc, my body suspended between momentum and gravity, I can just see him emerge on the far reach of the road again. Somewhere down the road he roars through a cloud of chickens; he has one now in his left hand; with a triumphant grin he twists the neck and drops it into the back seat with me. And I am swinging, and he is gone, and I hear only the creaking ropes and the rushing murmur of the moot of great pines above my head, and I do not let go the ropes and hurtle weightless into the horizon; instead, I sit down and hold tight to the ropes as the swing slowly, arc after arc, loses its force, drops slowly, arc by diminishing arc, to a penultimate gentle swaying to and fro, to and fro, until at last, imperceptibly but finally, dragging my feet in the dust, I am quiet, motionless, alone.

Icarus Ascending

Y FATHER WAS A sweet-natured man with many small skills and none of the great ones that would get him on in the world. His occasional heroic improvisations could deflect but never quite forestall our family's declining fortunes. We would shortly leave the collapsing little house among the pine trees, the last family ever to live there, and we would briefly perch in and remove from three other houses in as many years before finding our way into more permanent quarters in town. Uprooted from the home of my heart, and thrust too early into a knowledge of my father's mortality, through each successive change of home I carried in my heart a growing knot of apprehension, as though some looming catastrophe lay just over the horizon. Apprehension now congealed into a simple and continuing misery, and catastrophe contracted into mere entrapment, as we settled for seven years into the home of my humiliation. This period began in the summer of 1943 when I was eleven.

Our new home was a shabby gray house in a street of shabby houses backing up to the factory wall. It was a shotgun house—sixteen feet wide with living room, dining room, and kitchen in a straight row downstairs, two bedrooms and a bath above. In a sense, we had not lived so well for years: the house had a furnace and a gas cooking range and indoor plumbing if not hot water. But from our front door we looked out over a small dirt yard to the factory's cinder parking lot across the street, and from our kitchen wall to the factory wall was another bare ten feet of cinders. We awoke to the factory whistle rattling our windowpanes, and the saws whined through three shifts, day and night in the air about us like some degraded music of the spheres, until we noticed only the quiet of Saturday and Sunday. My father wallpapered the dingy living room, and one day a truck arrived with a sofa, an easy chair, and a big radio. But before long the wallpaper grew dim with coal smoke, and the cheap plush of the furniture wore off in patches.

That home itself, and all it represented, still tugs at me with a kind of profound gravitation, like a stellar black hole through which I might be sucked into oblivion. I dreamed vividly in those days. Some of those dreams still recur; others have passed and remain only as defining memories. I know I dreamed often of flying—literally soaring by waving my arms slowly like great pinions and exerting a kind of will to weightlessness; I remember the thrill and relief of those sleeping moments of freedom, floating above a dream landscape, and the sickening instant of free fall as my wings failed on waking.

II

My father called our location Zuber's Corner, because Charlie Zuber owned not only our house but the corner building next door as well, where he also collected rents from Ray Long's Corner Grocery and the apartments above it. This was a time when old Charlie Zuber and Long Ray Long circled over the landscape of my waking mind like dark birds in the sky. On the first of each month Charlie Zuber would descend, dropping into our living room to collect the rent. He was a short man in a dirty cap and an overcoat too large; a small cigar, damp and unlit, sagged in his stubble of beard. "You got some rent money for me, Mrs. Holtz?" he would ask, wheezing a little.

Sometimes my mother had his thirty dollars for him; sometimes she would have only twenty, or maybe a small roll of bills and some change.

"I'm sorry, Mr. Zuber, that's all I have now. I'll try to have more next time."

She would wait in embarrassed silence while he counted the bills and the coins. He would mutter to himself in German, suck his cigar, and cast reproachful glances around the room. From some inner pocket of his coat he would pluck a ragged account book and write out a receipt, marking always at the bottom a balance due. Once we had fallen behind, he would drop down on us at odd times during the month. "You got some rent money for me, Mrs. Holtz?" His accusing eye would catch mine, and I would writhe in vicarious guilt. Our furnace failed, and he would not repair it, so my father traded our dog Dick and his doghouse for a coal stove for the living room; the gas cooking stove heated the kitchen. One day our chimney caught fire and started a blaze on the roof. The fire company put it out quickly, but I was in a sweat of concern until I discovered that we would not have to pay for their visit or for the hole in Charlie Zuber's roof. My father patched the roof with a piece of tin. Charlie Zuber stood in the yard and eyed it for a while, then left, saying nothing.

My father called Ray Long Long Ray Long because he was a tall man, bald and skinny but potbellied. We owed him whatever we did not owe Charlie Zuber. He kept our grocery accounts in a small receipt book in a drawer with many others like it. My mother was encumbered with my sister and my brother, so I ran many errands for her. From time to time when I went for groceries, Long Ray Long would sack up the bread and milk and pork chops for me, look at our receipt book, and say very judiciously, "I think your mother better send some money with you next time. You tell her she needs to pay it down maybe ten dollars, okay?" Flushed with shame, I would slink home with the groceries and the message. Long Ray Long would get his ten dollars, but Charlie Zuber would be shorted again. Groceries were cheaper at the A&P downtown, and sometimes just after my father got a paycheck my mother would send me with a roll of bills and a list of staples. I was big enough to carry two shopping bags, but I had to come home through backyards and the back door, lest Long Ray Long see that we had taken our trade elsewhere. He was a decent man, I believe, who offered me rides home when he saw me on the street, but I could not meet him without guilt. And I'm sure Charlie

Zuber was entitled to all we owed him; I believe he carried us so long for fear he could rent that house to no one else. But he terrified me, creeping like a grimy shadow in and out of the shops downtown. More than once he would sidle up to me, wheezing faintly, as I stood on the street corner with my friends. "You tell your mother she got to have some rent money for me next time."

I ran other errands up and down the streets of town. With a small and diminishing roll of bills my mother handed me from her purse I paid our water bill and our light bill, and I paid the coal bill at the lumberyard. Sometimes I left a few dollars at Doctor Miller's office. And once each month I climbed the stairs to the office of the Franklin Finance Company where the mother of one of my friends sat behind a glass window to take my money. Eventually we paid for our sofa and chair and radio, but I knew that if we did not the man with the hook would take them away, as he had my father's car so long ago. My spirits rose and fell with the circumference of the roll of bills my mother handed me. "When your father's not at home, you have to be the man of the house for me."

My father was not at home much in these days, and there was seldom singing with the radio. He had left the factory even as we had moved within the shadow of its walls. His years on the factory floor, I now understand, had been an attempt to make a regular life with a family; but the work was wearing him down, and he needed a job that would strain his health less. He had earlier, from age eighteen, been an interstate truck driver, hauling new cars that he could never buy himself from the factories in Detroit to dealers throughout the Midwest. It was an irregular life, but it was sit-down work, and now he took up the trucker's life again, hauling miscellaneous freight over the same region for a local company instead. So for his remaining years I saw him mainly on occasional stopover visits.

Sometimes, when he needed someone to talk to to keep from falling asleep, he took me with him. They were exciting trips, roaring along the highway and looking down into the passenger cars below; there was a mystery and a craft to shifting through the many gears, navigating town to town, bypassing weigh stations through back roads, signaling oncoming trucks of lurking state troopers we had passed, backing huge trailers into narrow loading docks. There was a bunk at the rear of the cab; I would lie up there sometimes, sleeping and waking and half dreaming for long hours to the jostle of the road and peering out over my father's shoulder at the dark world rushing toward us in the glare of the headlights. Then it would be dawn, the road running off toward the first pink light, and we would stop for breakfast at some roadside diner and I would have pie and ice cream. He had to keep a log of his driving hours to prove to ICC inspectors that he took required intervals of rest; but the record was a fiction, and as he worked on it he called it his storybook. He had friends up and down the highways from years before, including toothless Tiny Middlehurst, who could chew beefsteak with his gums and who traveled with a little terrier that would drink whiskey from a saucer, and Parrot Smallwood, whose traveling companion was a stuffed parrot in a bell jar—once a live pet, it had eaten a match head and died. We would arrive at loading docks in the factory districts of Detroit or Chicago; crews of sweating blacks, or occasional whites—bohunks and polacks, they were called—who swore in strange languages, would unload and load cargo. The air was sharp with chemical smells and hazy with smoke, and I knew with some consolation that there were worse places to live than the home my father would take me back to. Twice, when I was not with him, he met with serious accidents. In Detroit, his truck was hit broadside by a streetcar and overturned; he was jailed and held for trial until fellow truckers took up a collection for his bail, and then charges were dropped. Near South Bend, an automobile driver fell asleep and swerved into his path; the driver was killed but my father was not hurt.

There was heroism in all of this, too; but I did not see it. He had to pass an annual physical to drive truck. Doctor Miller would listen to his chest and sign the papers reluctantly. "He says I should try to get a desk job," my father said, shaking his head and laughing. "I don't know . . . those pencils hurt my fingers." There came a time when he tried to buy a truck on terms from his company; he could then work as an independent operator and make more money. Or maybe even hire someone to drive for him. I remember a brief flurry of excitement as the idea took shape. "Maybe," he said to me, "in a few years I could get another truck and you could drive with me." I'm not sure he was

serious, but I wondered if I could ever learn the gears if I were called. He could not keep up the payments, though; the truck reverted to the company, my father continued to drive for hire, and my career as a trucker was aborted before I ever had a license to drive. I was left, however, with another dream that still comes back unbidden: I am young, alone in the cab of a great truck rushing down an empty highway at night; the steering wheel is in my hands but I have no control, and I do not know what lies in the dark beyond the small swath of light I push out ahead of me.

III

Beyond such occasional nightmares, though, more often I dreamed of flying. I dreamed of flying but I learned to march, and I still view my disciplined trek through adolescence as an astonishing spectacle. At the time, I did not know where the discipline came from, and perhaps I may say something of that further on. In many ways this was an ideal time and place to grow up. These were the years just after the Depression had ended and the war had been won, when the nation rode a great wave of optimism and prosperity. All things seemed possible, and the easygoing democracy of a small midwestern town posed few obstacles to anyone with ability and ambition. I have thought often about why my parents failed to thrive even modestly in these years, and all I can say is that long views seemed always to be obscured by pressing immediate circumstance. Perhaps they were so damaged by the early years of the Depression and the fears of the war that mere escape day by day into present safety was enough. Whatever the case, they were both incapable of the discipline necessary to begin by early small steps toward prosperity. My father could confront life with a jest and a song, and beyond those, short-term improvisations; my mother, having linked her fate to his, had already been worn down into passive acceptance. They were neither of them strong or clever, and the peril and disorder of their lives became apparent to me early.

But to speak of myself in these years gives me little pleasure, for I can tell merely the oft-told American story of the young man who, with ferocious precocity, raises himself by his bootstraps. I became, in my own way, strong and clever, but in the intervening years I have shed much of the arms and armor I fashioned for myself in those days, and that self I was I hardly know now, looking back on an abandoned husk.

I have lately attended a reunion of my old high school class. I had been to some early gatherings, but I had neglected them for thirty years; the gap is a measure of the discomfort I felt with the drama of my life in those high school days. I had been a select and honored member of that class, something of a paragon, indeed; but I had paid a price for those honors that I have not yet recouped, and I was reluctant to reenter an arena calling for skills I had long abandoned. But the evening went better than I feared.

With some of these people I went back to junior high school, where my verbal precocity had already marked me, and some of them were from my Boy Scout troop, where I had first discovered the satisfaction of winning honors in a progressive system of study and performance. I had been the youngest Eagle Scout in local memory, recognized at a banquet, where my mother, nervous in the glare of attention, pinned on my highest badge. With this momentum, I had entered high school with an alert eye for future glory, and I began my secret campaign to graduate at the head of my class. I was still reading voraciously, and I spent so much time at the library that I was given a job sweeping floors and shelving books, but I had no notion of literature as a calling, of learning as a profession. I was simply a scholarship boy, one of those deadly predators of knowledge for whom study is a contest to be won. I am sure that a certain religious boy, with a mind probably better than mine, and a certain quiet girl, a model student who took easier classes, had no idea what threats they seemed to me as I sized up my competition and glanced backward over my shoulder.

But this had been a private campaign, conducted during nights of study after I had put more important things behind me, for I was sensitive to the contempt for the merely brainy, and my successes had to appear as casual events that I took lightly; so the academic axis could not be the one on which I inserted, reasserted, myself among old friends that evening. It was fascinating to watch the old groupings sort themselves out at the tables and at the bar. There was no gathering of the merely brainy, no reminiscences of math tests or English classes; the religious boy, the quiet girl, my ancient rivals, were not to be seen, presumably having carried into vanquishment little emotional bond to their old classmates, while my place was defined by old bonds still in place. What turns over in my heart is the remembered passion of those bonds, the intensity of the daily smiling, cajoling assault by which I won and maintained a beachhead among the self-defined elite of these very ordinary people, among whom, so long ago, my love of the book and the word I concealed like a secret vice.

I simply needed to be admired, to be loved, I suppose, and I suspect that had I not been so seduced by books, and so humiliated by my life at home, I would have found mere normalcy an easy virtue. But instead I performed a daily dance of love that seemed to be the price of admission, with which I contrived for myself a place that I always felt was not mine by any right. If I could have been anyone, I would have been Gene Kelly, singing and dancing and smiling my way into people's hearts. No one had less aptitude for dance; but I found that I had my father's gift for entertainment—wit in conversation, bolstered with trivia from my reading and jokes borrowed from radio shows. I cultivated my "personality," convinced that it needed daily maintenance for a daily performance. I threw myself into dramatics and debate, operettas and choral singing, every club I had time for, and I studied the puerile politics of class elections, plotting annually with an inner circle over nominations and offices as part of another private master plan that would elevate me to student body president my senior year. I bruised and strained my body on athletic teams I had no talent for, just for the fellowship of those more gifted. These were the friends I gathered with for an evening after so many years, the old class officers, the jocks and cheerleaders, the simply popular, pleased to renew old friendships and melancholy with the reminders of the spent passions of youth.

What was it, really, I had wanted from them, beyond simple friendship, some validation of a place in the world? In a sense, I had wanted their homes, their families, and the natural confidence that came from such grounding. We were all middle class, I suppose; all of my friends came from blue-collar or white-collar families; but in the fine gradations of class and neighborhood of a small town, I felt an immense gap between my itinerant family in its grimy rented house and those disciplined enough to have risen to mortgaged homes, fixed addresses, and grassy lawns. Yet no one ever deliberately made me feel the shame that washed over me each night when I came home, and I value now the spontaneous goodwill of these friends in a way I could not then. They opened their homes and families to me, and to some of them I fastened almost parasitically, constructing a compound, interlocking surrogate family in place of my own.

And so we talked that night, years melting away into memories blurred smooth with many tellings by many tellers, and I went back again to Ray Long's Corner Grocery, which stood at the corner of Prospect Street, which ran out to the edge of town. The teller of this story was an auto mechanic, still a huge, muscular man of two hundred and sixty pounds, who used to brag that the toughest kids in town lived on Prospect Street, the tougher the farther out, and that he lived in the last house in the last block. He had been our premier athlete, faster and stronger than any of us, happy and sweet-tempered with all the good nature of an unchallenged champion, and he still gave me a sense of security by his mere presence. He had been the first among us to have his own car—first a Model T, then other salvaged wrecks he would dismantle and rebuild—and as we gathered in his driveway to hold tools and watch the progress of this sixteen-year-old mechanical prodigy, his mother took us all in at all hours of day and night. I did not live directly on Prospect Street, so I did not rate on the scale of tough, but I was on the margin, which was enough for me. Mornings, before school, I would wait at the corner of Prospect Street, and he would start at his end of the street and pick up his chosen few, one by one and finally me, in a ritual progress of retainers whose sense of majesty derived from honking at mere walkers on the way to school. One of his later cars was a 1929 Chevrolet he found stored in a farmer's barn. When he stopped to show it off, my father came out to admire it, and he laughed with all the knowledge of his experience with a '29 Chevy. "That'll be a pile of parts if you ever take it out of town, off a paved road," he warned. And we did take it out of town, on swimming trips by day and nighttime prowls along country roads to visit country girls and to steal watermelons and to raise hell generally. And the car did come apart, piece by piece, in a clattering reprise of the collapse of my father's car a decade before. It lost its headlights the night we drove across the state line to the Howe Military Academy, where we roared through the campus at midnight, honking and banging on the car doors and shouting, "The redcoats are coming! The redcoats are coming! To arms! To arms!" And now the driver pops another beer, shifting painfully on football-damaged knees, and recalls his mother's anger when he cleaned a carburetor in her sink. Dead for years now, he says, voice dropping, and in the silence of the moment I recall the driveway family she had sponsored with such grace.

Now it is the turn of another teller, an engineer with two hearing aids and, I know, a bridge replacing teeth he lost in football. His father had been a contractor, and his mother had taken me in like a second son in her small and tidy home. He and I had courted many girls together, one couple in the front and one in the back seat of his father's shining 1947 Chevrolet, on nighttime trips to basketball games, changing drivers on the return trip for the greater opportunities of back-seat bliss, or parked in some country lane, while the windows fogged over from the exhalations of passion during fumbling explorations of the rites of love. Or, at other times in rites no less important, three or four of us, young bucks womanless and lovelorn and predatory, shedding adolescence and rushing toward manhood, cruised the country roads by night, scattering beer cans in ditches and pausing to water steaming initials into the sand or yellow script into snowbanks, according to the season, and to howl at the moon. Or to gallop into mad gallantry, as when one Christmas vacation we discovered that a friend, a girl with no mother and an alcoholic father, had no Christmas tree. The answer, of course, was to steal one for her from a snow-covered lot, one evening when the knight-errant with his father's car, already too full of beer to drive it, stretched out on the floor of the back seat and moaned his misery. The snow-covered tree was jammed in on top of him, and as his father's car, now with the least-drunk driver, stopped at a red light downtown, he opened the back door to vomit into the street, thrusting his head and shoulders out from under the tree branches, a Christmas spirit of pathetic cheer. As the car pulled away from the light, he could see his mother, arms full of Christmas packages, watching him, her sick and sickening son, and her family car, driver unknown, heading east out of town on a mission of love. "God bless her," he says, mourning another mother, "she never said a word next day. Just asked me to clean the pine needles out of the car. Who *was* driving that night?" I remember, but he is dead now, long dead, dead too, too young, early promise cut short, and I fear to weep speaking his name.

But I do mention his name, only to praise his left-handed jump shot and his record, still standing, in the 440; and I tell another story, about someone else, because I do not think I can explain to them what I took away from my friendship with that least-drunk driver, as I edged myself, as far as I was able, into his large Catholic family in a large, orderly house. From father and mother down through seven children, these were attractive and self-confident people, and I could see the signs of their prosperity and discipline all about them, although it never occurred to me to wonder that they did not keep a car, and that they had rented out an apartment on their second floor. Their middle son, my special friend, suffered a hideous case of poison ivy one summer; he could not go out, and I spent many afternoons keeping him company in his itching isolation. Most of the time the family was gone; they led busy lives. In cool, well-kept, high-ceilinged rooms the two of us played checkers and cards and listened to brief, scratchy 78-rpm recordings on the phonograph; and I discovered music of a kind that had never come through the radio in my home, for this family had four classical recordings. I heard Tchaikovsky's *Romeo and Juliet,* Debussy's *Clair de Lune,* de Falla's *Ritual Dance of Fire,* and Gershwin's *Rhapsody in Blue.* I was stunned, disturbed, I could not believe that such gorgeous music had been hidden from me; over and over all summer while my friend scratched and suffered and daubed himself with calamine lotion, I played this family's poor little repertoire of concert showpieces, in a waking dream as compelling as any of those by night. When the family was at home the bustle made music impossible, but I hung around like a volunteer foster child, and they accepted me in good spirits. When they ate dinner I would not eat with them; their tacit closeness was an uncomfortable mystery to me. Instead, I sat in the backyard under a tree, and the mother brought out cake and ice cream at the meal's end and freed her son from the family table to keep me company.

Another teller tells another tale, and one by one we fall silent, old campaigners drifting toward somnolence and lurching to the bathroom as beer rises in the brain and settles in aging bladders; it is the hour when once we might have set forth to defy the world, standing shoulder to shoulder in the glare of headlights and the companionship of pissing contests with fire hoses able to tip a Coke bottle at ten feet. Now wives come to take us home to bed, and I am reluctant to leave, so taken am I again with these profoundly decent, ordinary people, whose long marriages and close families define my life as well. Certainly I had accomplishments they could never understand, and certainly I had changed in ways they could never imagine—ways that had brought the extraordinary young man who once performed among them to consider his ancient extraordinary self a simple garden-variety striver. What I found extraordinary now was the ready acceptance and affection that greeted me here. My accomplishments they found mildly interesting, but they were clearly and unaffectedly glad to see me. Had that extraordinary young man really been so successful in adhering himself to their hearts? Perhaps, I found myself reflecting, perhaps they might have given him their love had he never tried so hard. And what might he have done with his energies then?

And against homes like these, friends like these, against such attractions and temptations, against a life so filled with joy and passion and adventure and sheer normalcy, what chance did my parents have for my allegiance? For in these years I no longer traveled with my father, and my mother watched my comings and goings in silence.

I V

But there was more to my life than my life in school. As I edged into adolescence I emerged into an astonishing freedom. By twelve I was really beyond my parents' control, and by sixteen I had made several hitchhiking trips around the state with a tent and bedroll, always heading north. The release from my tensely structured life in school, and escape from the black hole of life beneath the factory wall, was my life in the lakes and woods of the surrounding countryside. The town was small, and once beyond it I wandered in a landscape still faintly edenic now, almost absolutely so then. A land sculptured by glaciers in ancient days had gentled into rolling fields and wooded hills cupping small lakes like jewels in a generous open palm.

It is hard in this fallen age to speak simply of these matters, for our latter-day sense of the natural world is complicated with deep ecological and philosophical concerns. And again, I can speak of the self I was only with a certain detached embarrassment, not because I have abandoned him but because he still persists in a vestigial innocence beneath the accreted layers of later knowledge that ought to have extirpated him. This young man had never read a nature writer; his immersion was in simple and unmediated pleasure. The trees still spoke to him, especially in the fall; he did not enjoy hunting, though he went with friends, and a day in the woods was often a day when he sat or walked without firing a shot. On a lake, or in it, though, he came alive in the simplest and most primitive way. He fished, I must say, fervently, religiously. The water's surface drew his gaze through a deceptive translucence into mysterious depths; his fishing line was a query, the tap and tug of some unseen creature a mute response, and the struggling rise of a hooked fish an excitement almost erotic. The fish out of water were always a disappointment; he cleaned them and took them home for the table as a duty, but with little pride or pleasure. But in the water, as he held them at boatside before landing, they were beautiful, full of portent he could never quite decipher.

And he became an adept swimmer, locally phenomenal for swimming underwater for long minutes at the lake bottom. Here was a flight and a dream of a different sort, before scuba gear, before even masks and snorkels, when with lungfuls only he could sink into a cool and silent realm, searching and searching for something, anything, whatever was there, hidden—hanging schools of bluegills that drifted off as he approached, a snapping turtle beneath a log, old fishing lures snagged on brush piles—until the blood pounded in his ears, his vision blurred, and strangling for air he had to burst to the surface and breath. Truly, it seemed that drowning might be a small price to pay for such hidden knowledge. At night in his bed he practiced holding his breath to gain greater endurance, and he sank toward anaerobic unconsciousness and an elusive dream, until his lungs reasserted their claim and he gasped to life again. He was fascinated to find in his biology class that he had once had fetal gills; and he found in an old *Esquire* magazine a haunting fantasy of a boy born with such gills, swimming underwater until he was transformed into a fish.

Most of my early dreams have left me, but I still dream at times of a secret lake, a hot and windy day as I float its surface in my boat, over and over a thrilling pull at my line trailing in its depths. Or, from a high bank I look down into water where great lurking shapes move in slow undulations to some secret purpose. And long before I thought of professional ambitions, of marriage and a home of my own, of anything like a normal life, I carried embedded thoughts of a life lived permanently on the verge between a wooded hill and a still lake, dawn breaking quietly over rising mists. Later, reading Jung, I find that I have been pressing the barrier between the conscious and the unconscious, which I am willing to believe, and willing to leave the matter there.

V

Needless to say, my life in these years was a tacit judgment on my parents. How shameful it is to be ashamed of one's home and parents, how doubly shameful to be ashamed of the shame! In the little house among the pines I had felt no shame, but that had been in my age of innocence. Now I saw with a different eye, and in these years I came to blame my father for all that he lacked. I once thought bitterly that if he had carried me further, like the diligently supportive fathers of some of my friends, I would not have started so far behind. Much that I came to understand about him I understood condescendingly as a kind of permanent adolescence, an irresponsible failure to grasp the terms the world had offered him. I grasped those terms early, and it hurts me now to think how puzzling I must have been to him as I orbited into worlds he could never enter.

A family joke persists between me and my children and grandchildren: that I was never a little boy, that I was always a little man. I am not sure when the joke started, but I locate it somewhere in my recognition, too early, of the pressures that weighed on my parents. I suspect that the books and magazines I absorbed at such a prodigious rate had given me an ill-sorted precocity of vision against which my parents stood little chance. Step by step I took my own life in hand and separated it from theirs. I still remember with guilt each dime and dollar they spent on me in moments when they could; my job at the library gave me a margin of independence, and summers I was a caddy at the country club. Soon I was largely self-supporting except for my bed and an occasional meal at home. I took personal charge of my neglected health. At age twelve I decided that the swelling in my jaw was from an abscessed tooth and took myself to the dentist to have it pulled. At seventeen I tired of my constant sore throats and scheduled my own tonsillectomy; Doctor Miller scraped them out in the back room of his office, Doctor Gillespie assisting with the ether cone; and a friend took me home, still woozy, in a borrowed car. At that time I had a part-time job in a shoe store. My father had scoffed at my job lugging clubs for the swells at the country club, who were, he said, just trying to hit a little ball without hitting the big one. But something subtle and defining happened when I blossomed into white shirts and gorgeous ties to clerk in a store. His derision was good-natured but clear-sighted. "Well," he grinned, "it's inside work, and no heavy lifting."

My parents, of course, understood very little of my life. I told them only of results, nothing of the work and calculation. My parents knew my friends by report alone because I did not ask them into my home; they would come in cars and I would be waiting at the curb; sometimes I would ask to be dropped off blocks away and walk home. I told my parents nothing of my girlfriends, although my mother, I suspect, plied my sister for information. I had shut my family out of my life, and how were they to deal with me but not to stand in my way?

One of my jobs at home was to fill and empty the washing machine on laundry day. I would first fill, bucket by bucket, the wash boiler on the kitchen stove, then bail hot water, bucket by bucket, into the washer. When the washing was done, I would drain the dirty water, bucket by bucket, and pour it down the kitchen sink. I was draining water one day when I looked up at my mother standing in the doorway and realized that she was pregnant.

I was sixteen then; she would soon be forty. I had already decided that my parents had botched their lives badly, but I had been able to project better years ahead for them, as I would clear space at bed and table by leaving home, and my sister would shortly follow. I could not believe they had been so utterly foolish now. And it was another embarrassment from my home; my friends' mothers, even some of the Catholics, had all left off childbearing at a decent age; two children, except for Catholics, was the ideal; indeed, the prosperity and decency of their homes had depended on this kind of prudence. Indeed, my own caution in matters sexual was already firmly in place: my life

"I fell in love with the girl I would marry, but I did not know this yet."

could be spoiled, I saw clearly, by a hasty pleasure that could trap me in an early marriage. I did not then see the ironic reversal of roles, as in my heart I wept with shame at my parents' folly and in my mind lectured them on family planning. All of this settled on me in an instant as soapy gray water filled the bucket between my feet.

Not a word was mentioned to me as the weeks progressed, and I was too humiliated to say a word. My brother was born in March, and to my credit he found a place in my heart. I threw myself into my last year of school with a redoubled intensity. I was elected student body president by a satisfying majority over my rival. I graduated at the head of my class of ninety-six students, beating out my religious rival and the quiet model student by perilously thin margins. I won three college scholarships. I fell in love with the girl I would marry, but I did not know this yet. I rolled through the final weeks of school in a blaze of triumph and glory, having raised myself

Summer 1950: my newest brother and I,
and the factory at the back of our house.

ex nihilo to a peak at eighteen that I could only descend from for the rest of my life. My parents attended my graduation, heard my valedictory speech, and stood smiling and ill at ease as the principal asked them to rise for special recognition for producing such a paragon. As we left the gymnasium, strangers congratulated them and me. My father's black derby hat, by now a little greasy and spotted, stood out as a curious affectation in a sea of gray and brown fedoras. And in my moment of greatest triumph, my humiliation was also complete, for my mother was obviously, almost terminally, pregnant again.

My third brother was born a month before I went off to college. My father had discovered another car, a 1941 Hudson, that bordered on respectability, and in that he and my family carried me up to the university, my parents and the two babies in the front seat, my sister, my brother Roger, and I cramped together in the back. I remember saying, self-consciously gallant, that they would have more room on the way home; certainly I knew that they would have more room in the house. My father helped me carry my trunk and suitcase up to my dormitory, and then we walked back to the parking lot, where my mother had laid out a small picnic lunch on the hood of the car. I ate peanut-butter sandwiches and drank lemonade and wished urgently for them to leave. My newest brother soiled his diaper, and my mother stood at the open car door, changing him on the front seat. "Bill, we better go," she said to my father. "This is the baby's last diaper."

My father smiled uncertainly at me. He wore his derby hat and his good suit, and in these years he had taken to wearing a navy blue shirt with a yellow tie, so that he looked faintly like a movie gangster. He shook my hand vigorously. "Well, son," he said, "keep your nose clean. Don't take any wooden nickels."

It was the only advice he had ever given me. I watched them drive out of the parking lot into the street and then I walked up into the dormitory to find my new life.

VI

It is tempting to end this account here, like a work of fiction, marking a sharp boundary between stages of my life. But life itself is more nearly a matter of torn pages and ragged edges. And there is little that need be said about my university life except that it went well: I had found where I belonged, and I began another long march. But the good-byes to my family went on and on.

I came home from my first year of college to find my family evicted from the little house next to the factory walls. "For the time being we're living at the county farm," my mother had written to me during my exams. The old county farm, four miles from town, had been since the nineteenth century the home of last resort for the aged poor. Like a red brick baronial mansion, it stood well back from the highway, behind a circular drive and a great lawn with stately trees; but inside it was a crumbling ruin. Lately it had been closed and abandoned for several years; ownership had reverted to a pair of bachelor farmer brothers; and my father, in another of his remarkable expedients, had struck a deal to move his family temporarily into the great central dormitory. I arrived to find my mother and father, my sister and my younger brothers, encamped in the cavernous and echoing kitchen. A lobby, a dining hall, and a parlor, all institution-sized, completed the ground floor; overhead, in separate men's and women's wings, were thirty or so bedrooms, one of them mine for the time being. Here, at least, we were not crowded.

I had long struggled with embarrassment at the conditions of my family life; now I found myself beyond embarrassment: all of this, I told myself, had nothing to do with me. At the bottom of the present distress, of course, was a question of unpaid rent. I remember the local sheriff visiting for a quiet talk with my father in the driveway. While I watched from my window, I could see my father work a charm: an ingratiating grin, a disarming jest, an evasive story, until the sheriff was nodding and smiling and the men shook hands in a backslapping farewell in which nothing had been decided. I had seen the style before, and in a moment of revelation I recognized the model of my own strategic style, with which I had slipped and dodged my way through the social demands of high school and which was already serving me well in college. My father had paid his way through much of his life with that coin, and already so had I; but I was beginning to have serious doubts about the authenticity of my engagement with the world, and only years later would I think to ask what inner terrors my father had evaded with his charm.

I hitchhiked back and forth to a summer job at the creamery in town. With each ride—once with one of my old girlfriends, still friendly—I had to explain the little colony I lived among at the old county farm, and I found that I had my father's skill to cope.

Before the summer was over, my mother approached me for a loan from my college savings. I gave it gladly, and a small roll of bills passed from my hand to her purse; for two hundred dollars I was buying my freedom, and Charlie Zuber was exorcised forever. My friends, home from college, came out to visit me, and without evasion, but with an ironic consciousness of my prospects and my family's fallen state, I showed them around the caverns and crannies of my new home. By the time my parents reestablished themselves in their next home, their last and the fourteenth that I could remember, I came as a visitor.

Not long after, I was money ahead enough to go shopping for my own first car. I took my father along, and together we found a beauty that put a gleam in his eye and envy in his voice. It was a 1937 Pontiac, an eight-cylinder sedan of faded but still discernible elegance. My father walked around it, caressing its fenders as he might the backside and breasts of a once-lovely woman. "Oh, they was great cars back in '37. They ain't been this good since the war. When I was hauling cars for the White Star line, I used to deliver these sweethearts to the dealerships all around Michigan and Ohio." I was trying to calculate what girls in Ann Arbor I could get into that car with me.

The price was a hundred and twenty-five dollars; I had the money in my pocket but my father did not. We started for home in two cars. Ahead of me, my father's car was stuck in second gear; I put my foot to the floor and accelerated around him, honking with my new horn while he waved and grinned. On the highway behind me I watched him grow smaller and smaller in my mirror until he disappeared in a dip in the road.

Brother's Keeper

*M*Y BROTHER NOW IS DEAD. His fifty-one years, through which he fled us all, day by day, down his tangled path of failure and pain, ended in this last evasion, and the few of us who gathered in the October rain in a raw new cemetery, scarce distinguishable from the pastures surrounding, were dry-eyed. Nature might weep its annual lament, but for us grief had run its course long ago. What remains when grief is gone is grief's shadow, a void our baffled and defeated care had left that the formal ritual of burial could not exorcise.

I have written earlier of how, on a December night while the sky blazed with the aurora borealis, my grandmother and I ushered my brother into the world; and of how, as a rocking chair rhythmically rode forward against falling darkness while I held my brother to my heart, she and I sang away the terrors of the world. Would that a song could last for all time! But some lives are at best broken music, and our cradlesong remained too frail a melody to carry beyond that moment in the lamplight of a winter-bound kitchen. *Oh, Grandmother, help me now!* For my brother now is dead, and I do not know what song to sing to fill the ragged vacancy in my heart.

Nor do I know what the altered music might have been to save him. What I do know now is that already in his early years I was shaping myself for an escape from the shabby disorder of our family life, a journey that required a marching tune I gradually discovered. I can now look back with sorrow and regret and, finally, even with forgiveness to my parents, whose fumbling good intentions were regularly undercut by their weaknesses and the terrific strains of the Great Depression and the Great War that followed. But in those years I was driven by fear and anger and, so unfairly, by a resentment of their inadequacies; and as I found a way so different from theirs—so clear and simple, it seemed to me in my easy arrogance—much was left behind. Among those abandoned fragments of a life gradually stripped of its own origins were, I weep to say, my brother and the boy's clear voice with which I eased his sleep. The voice is cracked with neglect and age, and my brother now is dead.

I I

From what remnants might I compose my song? A few surging images from memory, but without continuity. A few documents: some letters, not to me; a yellowed page still curled from a typewriter; a handful of photographs. I find a picture of him, taken on his fourth birthday, I recall.

December 9, 1943. In those days a traveling photographer would pass through town from time to time, rent a room at the hotel that he converted to a temporary studio, and advertise in the local paper for portraits. I remember the mingled fuss and distraction of the occasion because my brother's birthday came just days after the anniversary of the Japanese attack on Pearl Harbor. We are two years into the midst of the war; the local newspaper carries an extensive account of the occasion, which I sit reading as my brother poses; and my father, who has written his draft number in grease pencil on the rearview mirror of our car, is joking tensely with the photographer about going to Japan.

The photographer summons me to stand in one corner of the room, a yellow balloon aloft in my hand. "A balloon for you, buddy," he coaxes my brother, "if you can give us a great . . . big . . . smile."

Against a painted sylvan backdrop my brother sits gazing toward me,

one leg crossed under him, hair
damply combed, resplendent in
a sailor suit and a shining smile
that smites my heart with the
delayed force of five decades. It
is a smile that will in time
regularly open hearts, doors, and
pockets to him. Now, in this
moment, I am completely yours,
it promises; I will do anything
to please you; take me to you
and I will be all you hope I can
be . . . The shutter clicks; my
brother rushes to hug my waist
and reach for his balloon; guns
roar across the world; my father
does not go to war; and my
brother smiles his promise forev-
er from the shelves, dressers, and end tables of the various homes we will
drift through year by year.

III

My brother now is dead, and at the back of my mind is the mutter of
distant thunder.

My brother and I sprang from the same seed, and if I have puzzled
over any one thing more than another about our family, it has been
over the play of fate and luck and will that has so far sheltered me
while raining destruction down upon my brother. Character is destiny,
we can say in pride or despair, but our genes can substitute for either
term in that old equation. In another determinism, we would dissolve
the quaint and more ancient idea of fate into mere history, but however much we acknowledge the great massed forces that move in slow
rhythms through our lives, we live our days in breaths and heartbeats
and poignant hypotheses of personal moment, and fate emerges from
history as we glance back over our shoulders. Certainly, though the

flow of time has afforded me a protected passage denied my parents, I have often flattered myself on shaping my course toward a few simple goals—in the midst of easy blandishments and leaping fears merely choosing my own clear path.

Yet in my heart of hearts I long ago discounted all; as I glimpse the tiny margin for choice in the whirl of chance and necessity it often seems that I am merely free on parole, and fate breathes on my neck. First choices were already made for me, as chance brought two flawed people together in a flare of passion, and in my parents' bed was set in motion the spiraling double-helix dance of chromosomes, sorting from myriad possibilities those that were mine alone. In that tiniest of dances I see compressed a figure for the vastest whirlwind of fate, coiling and uncoiling from out of the past, across the landscape of our lives, and into the horizon of our time to come. What are the eruptions in history of the random mutations, the chemical assaults, the bombardments of cosmic radiation that flicker like lightning in the heart of the storm and shift destiny in the molecules of our cells? The dull murmur at the edge of my consciousness is the distant roar of fate, and each day as the storm gathers at my back I choose and choose and choose.

A voice from out of the whirlwind asks me about my brother, who now is dead, and I do not know how to reply. I, who have given him as hostage, seek the easy answer: forgive me, I was not there.

I V

My brother now is dead, although I, who am still living, led him into life by an advance of seven years; and I find I cannot speak of him without speaking of myself as well. My steps in those days were already reflective and cautious, as I separated myself from the unreflective and provisional expedients of my family life. But before he could reflect, before caution was even possible, my brother's life was marked for doctors' care and dangers to his flesh. At this remove, it seems an obvious and easy explanation.

February 1940. In his first winter the doctor arrives to treat a bad case of croup, but my mother is equally concerned with a mark since birth on his breast.

"What do you think of this?" she asks, tracing her finger over a strange whorl of skin and flesh that seems tender as she presses it.

The doctor probes with his fingers; it is an adhesion, harmless, he tells my mother, and the mark remains through later years, white and hairless and untanned.

Summer 1941. Later, as my brother gains his feet and wobbles out into the world, my earliest memories are of rescuing him from the highway. We are in a different house by this time, one set back by a long yard from the state highway that leads to our town. In these wartime years, cars are held to a speed limit of thirty-five, and few travel much faster, but the danger is real as my brother turns his unsteady steps, time after time with aggravating persistence, toward the humming road. I am supposed to watch him as I sit reading on the porch. Withdrawn into my book, I yet have to read with a marginal consciousness of danger; suddenly I look up to see my brother a hundred feet away, lurching and stumbling through the grass and rising to lurch roadward again. Then the frantic dash to tackle him on the verge of the gravel shoulder and lead him back to safer regions at the rear of the house, where sometimes he can be distracted to play in the dirt at the edge of the garden and I might lean against the corner of the house, one eye on him and the other on my abandoned book.

Summer 1942. By the next summer my father has fenced in the yard with chicken wire stretched between the trees. My brother is safe in his earliest prison; but I am free, unconcerned as the cars whiz by and he leans longingly against the fence, gazing out at the forbidden road until his face and forehead bear the hexagonal wire-marks of his confinement. By that time he is old enough to play with me in some ways, and we discover a game that gives him giggling glee and me—well, what? At this remove, I can hardly say, except that I connect it with my earliest sense of companionship and concern.

The porch is shoulder height to me, with narrow steps ascending, and my brother stands on the first step and jumps down, and then from the second another leap all the way down and an unsteady landing. On the third he faces me at eye level, but the jump is more than he dares try.

I hold out my arms to him. "Come on, jump. I'll catch you."

He leaps and I catch him to my chest and slide him to the ground, and as he chuckles in delight we repeat the jump again and again. Then he leaps from the fourth step, and from the fifth, fearlessly. With each higher step he hits my arms and chest with greater force, staggering me, until, with a triumphant crow, he launches himself confidently from the porch itself and I reach to catch him. The misstep and misjudgment are wholly mine, as his forehead hits my nose and we collapse to the ground together in a welter of my blood and his cries of fright and pain.

A grinding guilt dogs me for days. My brother's trust is untarnished, however, as he remounts the steps and stands with his arms outstretched to me, smiling. "That boy is a slow learner," my father says, laughing, telling the incident over to my uncles one by one. I honestly do not know how soon the next event follows, or even if they are connected by anything but the terrified howling, as for a whole day my brother lies rigid in his bed, screaming with pain until my father comes from work and rushes him to the hospital. He is home that evening, smiling contentedly and eating ice cream and wearing a small truss for a hernia low down upon his groin. "The doctor says he was probably born with it," my father reports to my mother. "Any little strain could have opened it up."

For years as I hold him I can feel the truss beneath his clothing; it is the first thing he puts on every morning, unless he forgets, and we have to chase him down to install it. In time the rupture heals naturally, though, and the truss is abandoned. Years later he has all but forgotten it until I mention it to him. And he, who now is dead, could remember nothing of the leap into space when I had reached to catch him and had failed.

Another easy answer: my brother trusted others too much, himself not at all.

V

My brother now is dead, and although I led him into the world by an advance of seven years, and we lived together for a decade under the same roofs and slept sometimes in the same bed, precious little of his life comes to recall as I rummage in those years. I suspect that it is not so much that I have forgotten as that I never noticed, self-absorbed and already arcing out into my eccentric orbit. Was he perhaps, driven by an endowment darker than my own, already wandering into his own orbit, more regular and more deadly? By the time he was seven and I fourteen his world was marked not by books and Hitler but by television and the mushroom cloud.

Thus I ransack history for blame and explanation. For that war of my childhood has been called the last good war, while his dawning awareness could be only of the madness of all war and the generality of guilt. And while I understand that my nature was early and permanently transformed by books, I recognize that few born after me could develop in such innocence. As he grew into his childhood and I into my adolescence, such were the markers that divided me from my brother, who now is dead.

Summer 1946. Our family has moved three times more by now, and we are living in town in the dingy house hard by the factory walls. The first television set in our neighborhood is owned by a radio repairman who lives on the corner across the street from us. In the long summer evenings most kids play in the street or in the factory parking lots rather than in the tiny yards of the huddled homes. As darkness falls, the street lamps come on, which is the general signal to head for home, and often as not my brother is missing. My mother sends me to find him, and often as not I know just where to look. Across the street on the corner, on the large front porch of our neighbor's house, a small figure stands in the gathering darkness. When I reach him I can see that he stands with his face pressed against the window. Inside, on the eight-inch screen, flickers Ed Sullivan or Milton Berle or grotesque professional wrestlers. My brother looks up only when I put my hand on his shoulder.

"Wait a minute," he says, "I want to see this." And I wait until the next commercial before leading him home. I have saved him from the highway, but no chicken-wire fence can preserve him from the absorption of consciousness by a fluorescing screen onto which all the trivial and terrible images of our time will emerge daily. My brother, who now is dead, is our family's first modern child, while I am the last of an older order.

My own life was largely under my own control by then. Part-time jobs supplied most of my wants, and except for a place to sleep and occasional meals I was independent of my parents. Despite occasional awkward gestures toward guidance they seemed content with the arrangement, although I now understand that they simply had no way of dealing with a precocity and will directed toward ends they could not envision. These were the days when my father had returned to work as an interstate truck driver and was seldom at home, and in his absence I seemed to occupy by default the vacated position of privilege. I was, I suppose, in a sense a neglected child; but I had adopted myself to raise by my own standards, and I owed many minor debts of adoption to the parents of some of my friends, whose more comely lives I admired. It was quite clear to me that my gift with books would get me somewhere, although the goals were indistinct. Those fine social gradations of a small-town society were achingly distinct, however, as I edged my way into that group in which I paid my way with that studied wit and charm modeled on my father's, but elevated a notch or two from my reading. I was genuinely admired, I believe, by my friends, who could not comprehend my academic gifts but who found me an entertaining good fellow nonetheless. My terror was ever to let them know how hard I worked nights before exams. Or ever to have to invite them into my home. This was, in short, my period as a precocious snob and prig already accelerating rapidly out of my origins. I was also, I thought, marking a path and establishing a momentum for those behind me. I could see my sister, two years behind me, progressing nicely. And I could see my brother struggling, although I did not know how or why, and my brother now is dead.

Any time 1946–1950. Where are the shining report cards my sister and I generate as a matter of course? I am humiliated by the mediocrity that his cards document and I counsel with my mother about it. The teachers complain that he understands his work but is easily distracted; books are lost or forgotten, homework undone. He reads fluently and with understanding beyond his years, but only what pleases him. I help him with his math assignments for a while. He works diligently while I am at his elbow, mastering the material easily, and his smile is luminous with gratitude for the attention, but left to himself he simply stalls. One teacher says that my brother has set a record for lost workbooks.

He is left-handed, a bar sinister across his days at school, for an early teacher has tried to force him to write with his other hand. He struggles to please, and for a while he can print his name equally well with either hand, but in later years, self-conscious about the unformed scrawl he writes, he will joke that school has left him ambidextrous, unable to use either hand well. On the playground his schoolmates complain that a left-handed batter is hard to pitch to, so he obligingly switches to the other side. In my superior knowledge, I explain the shortened route to first base and the advantages of lefties against right-handed pitching, and he cheerfully stands against the garage door, swinging left-handed as I lob balls to his bat. But on the playground, anxious to please, he reverts. Neither sinister nor dexterous, my brother is a left-hander in a right-handed world.

Eventually, long after it was too late to help me in my ministrations—if even such knowledge could have helped—I began to understand how I had spoiled the world for him as I pursued my own parochial glory. In a town and school that would also have to be his matrix, I was setting deadly standards for him to aim at. By the time I left high school my scrapbook and my ego bulged with accumulated certificates of honor. I was, in short, a classic American type, a young man of parts, all of them fabricated; and I trust that it is an authentic modesty that now blushes at the recital. In the year that I left home, my brother labored in the fifth grade under a teacher who had taught both me and my sister. She pulled his hair and tweaked his ear at his shortcomings. Daily measurement against such paragons could only exact a lethal toll, and I can believe how easily he could begin to fabricate himself as not the same but as the other, so cast in my shadow as to make that shadow his substance, fated to become—or to make himself—a dark figure of all I could never be. Looking back, I could see only the pathway marked for him to follow. Looking forward, what could he see but hurdles to stumble at, unless he could find some way around? He has not stumbled, however, at the final hurdle, but has vaulted far ahead of me, for my brother now is dead.

September 1949. In the autumn of my last year in high school I am with friends at the county fair. We are standing in front of the Tilt-a-Whirl, considering a ride. I feel a tug at my arm. It is my brother, hot and dirty and grinning to discover me. "Take me with you," he pleads.

He has spent his money, a few dollars from my mother, mostly on a wheel-of-fortune in hopes of winning an Indian blanket. "I can't," I say. The ride is fifty cents; I have a dollar and change; and it will be a week before I have more. He persists. "C'mon. Take me with you."

I push him away. "No, you can't come with me." I give him a dime. "Go get yourself a candy bar. Get lost."

From the whirling ride I can see him in the crowd below me for a few revolutions before I lose track. When I come down to the ground he is gone.

VI

My brother now is dead, and I can remember so little of his later years because I knew so little to remember. From the time I left home, the hours I would spend with my brother would, I fear, not fill a week.

He would never attend the university, which was, of course, my natural element, where I quickly learned to swim in its waters. Presently my sister joined me there, finding her own way to what she needed from that world. My brother was now the oldest at home, and might have profited from the focused attention of my parents had they not, to my chagrin, carelessly brought two more children into the world during my last years in high school. I was truly gathering momentum toward a different life now, and except for brief moments during my visits home my brother had slipped beneath the horizon of my attention, although I still assumed that he would in time find his way to the clearly marked channels I had traveled.

November 1952. I go looking for him one afternoon during a weekend at home. My mother suggests I try the bowling alley. It is unfamiliar territory for me, a hangout for factory-league teams and a loose collection of lowlife types. Through the crowd I spot him at a pinball machine. He is in junior high by now, bulky and overgrown for his age; he sees me almost as I see him, and the smile he casts me is spontaneous good cheer. I think I see him drop a cigarette as I make my way toward him, but I can not be sure. He introduces me to his friend, a grimy boy with a mop of tightly curled hair and an accent from the South, and it strikes me that he is genuinely proud I have come looking for him. And excited to share his plans: Duane's father is a preacher, but his mother is a waitress who sometimes sings at The Boot, a hillbilly bar outside town; Duane's father is taking them out to a rehearsal before the bar opens. "And you should hear her yodel! She's as good as any of them singers on the National Barn Dance."

I wince—at his low grammar, low companion, low taste. I have just discovered Mozart, have just bought my first record player and first LP records. For Christmas I buy my brother a recording of Prokofiev's Peter and the Wolf.

Shall I catalog his crimes against me in the years of his adolescence? In no particular order. My hunting knife borrowed and lost. My camping tent borrowed and torn. My father's twelve-gauge double-barrel, which ought to have been mine, clumsily sawed off to make a brush gun. For one Christmas I gave him my rifle; I have it now, useless without the bolt and clip that he left in some friend's car. He joined the Boy Scouts but never earned a badge. He went out for the freshman football team but did not finish the season. He played a little softball, and still batted right-handed. He bought a guitar and imitated Elvis Presley. He was hopeless, and now he is dead.

September 1953. One summer I leave my typewriter at home while I work in the mountains of Idaho. On my return I find it in his room with a sheet of paper rolled in:

> One night as I was going to bed a strange ring of red and green lights went zooming past my window.
>
> Hay I said to myself, whats that?
>
> I looked out and saw a strange saucer shaped aircraft in the backyard. As I watched a door opened and a strange creature stepped out.

And there it stops. A thin coating of dust has already settled on the keys, and as I pull the paper out it curls and I can see that it has started to discolor. And the keys are jammed. His smile always disarms my anger, and there is nothing I can say. I have recently read a story of alien invaders and their protection of a new race of mutant humans, preternaturally brilliant and gifted children. For his birthday I give my brother a copy of Arthur C. Clarke's Childhood's End.

VII

My brother now is dead because his daily pain required a nightly numbness that was the price of sleep, because the anesthetic fog concealed the contours of his grief, because he was a drunk.

My family had always lived one paycheck ahead of poverty and sometimes, as my father was out of work, several paychecks behind it. But when my father's heart failed him and he began a slow decline toward death, and my mother went to work in a toy factory, leaving him at home to care for the children, the precarious order of the new arrangement failed my brother. He resented my enfeebled father's querulous authority, and when I saw him he was sullen and evasive. He was finding his own life somewhere, but he was unwilling to talk about it. I was in the Army then, far away and starting my own family, and I saw these other troubles as through the small end of a telescope. My brother was seventeen when my father died; during my brief leave for the funeral, I tried to assume some authority as the shattered family passed through the ritual, and I found my brother balky and uncooperative, and he shed no tears. In the time that followed, my mother coped as best she could, and finally well enough, with the younger children, but my brother was already beyond her. The reports that reached me suggested someone strangely prone to accident: he rode his bicycle into a parked car and broke a collarbone; he fell down the basement stairs. Only as I write these lines does it occur to me that he was perhaps already finding comfort in a bottle. In the next year he dropped out of high school, and my mother was ashamed to tell me.

My brother was a shadowy figure beyond my reach now, although I tried several hortatory letters, which went unanswered. My sister was teaching high school in a small town in another part of the state. Her effort at rescue was to invite him to live with her and finish his last year of school. She reported him to be a good student, an excellent baby-sitter with her little girl, a congenial classmate with his new peers. "But what was his problem?" I asked, still seeking the easy formulation. "In twenty-five words or less."

"Drink," she said. "Shall I repeat it twenty-four times? We bailed him out of the county jail. It ended his chances at the school."

He returned home to live with my mother and enrolled in a special program meant to give students like him a second chance. Really it was his third, one more cut at the ball in a game designed for those who would swing from the right side of the plate. He reached a point at which only one course stood between him and graduation. The night before his final examination, he was jailed for driving drunk. This time my mother bailed him out.

I have a letter he wrote my sister's family shortly afterward; he was working nights in a factory.

> Dear everybody,
>   I just got home from my night of bonded slavery. My work is simple, boring, and uninteresting, so I am doing quite well at it. As everyone predicted, I regret not returning to school, but I am not spending a lot of Mom's money.
>   I bought a car (a '37 Ford coupe that is) a month or so ago and have been spending my spare time tinkering with it, which

is my excuse for not writing sooner.

Well, I am getting a mite sleepy, so I think I'll close now and
go to bed.

Lately I have learned that he made a trip to a distant town to visit
my cousin's husband, a vocational arts teacher in a community college. "Obviously, your brother wanted to get his life in order," he
told me. "He wanted to know what he could do without a college
degree. He was interested in trade apprenticeship programs. He said he
was out of step and wanted to get back in line." My brother had his
own easy formulations.

He was batting in a new ball game now. My mother posted bail for
him three times for DWI arrests. The third time he faced a felony conviction and prison time. My mother gave him a little money, and he
skipped bail and went to Kentucky. But eventually he returned, forgiven or forgotten by the law; I could never find out. And now, for
sure forgotten if not forgiven, my drunken brother is dead.

VIII

My brother now is dead because perfidious flesh functions without a
warranty, because the replication of his patrimony was a perfect imper-
fection, because he was born with my father's doomed heart.

At about this time, early in my professional career, I began to accept
my brother's perversity as a reversion to type of my father's feckless
family. My mother's family had produced several college-educated
professionals, and although she had not risen to that standard, I could
posture myself as a continuation of that line. My father's family, eleven
siblings, were factory hands and the like and, in their daily presence in
my early life, seemed chiefly preoccupied with visiting each other,
joking and talking and eating and drinking in a jovial solidarity of
the mediocre; in my horde of cousins I felt myself to be a kind of
changeling. At some point, in a flaming injustice, I discovered I could
overcome my humiliation at such a lineage by a simple betrayal of
those good people, preening in the greater luster I gained against so
dim a background. The inheritance I feared from my father was his

heart; several of his older brothers had dropped in middle age just as he had, and as I sought traces of his body in my face and frame a worm of fear gnawed in my breast. My brother, I began to feel, was in his improvidence truly my father's son; and when occasions arose to re-count my origins, I brought forward, with patronizing irony, my father and my brother as implicit foils to my own life. And surely jus-tice would assign the frailty of the family malady to my brother and not to me. He was called up for military service, only to be rejected for some anomalous murmur in the chambers of his heart. Lightning had struck from out of the storm, but I was not there.

I X

My brother now is dead, but he was a long time dying. Molecule by molecule death was accumulating in his veins while my life rolled smoothly on, and for almost a decade I did not see my brother.

At my class reunion a friend mentioned having stopped to help him change a tire in a driving rain: "Drunk as a skunk. I just put him in my truck and took him home." I heard of him at various jobs in Florida and North Carolina; he was a pipeline welder, my mother said.

October 1968. And suddenly he shows up to visit me in California; he is working in Los Angeles and living on the beach in Venice. What new sus-ceptibilities can he have discovered in lotusland? He is reticent about his personal life, but it is a curious relief to meet him as an adult, a pleasant, smiling young man about whom I need no longer worry, who delights my children as their newly emerged uncle. We spend an afternoon laughing and talking on our patio, eating watermelon and spitting seeds, and then he is gone again.

"I'll come and see you," I volunteer.

"Better not." He is evasive; he has no fixed address, no telephone yet. Watermelon vines sprout among the dichondra in my yard and I hear no more from him.

July 1970. A few years later we intersect again as I visit my old hometown and find him married, stepfather to a little boy from his wife's first marriage, and about to become a father himself. Or so the appearances and allegations. The woman is young and pretty and, for all the attention I can elicit from her, apparently from another planet. Later I learn that she is simply a tramp, that there has been no marriage, although the second child seems to be genuinely my brother's. So proud he is, in his simulation of a conventional domestic arrangement! And for a while I am hopeful that he has found his way into the world again; but the arrangement soon collapses, the woman departs with his child, and my brother wanders off again to take up a relationship for some years with a woman in North Carolina.

Here was happiness if ever he was to know it—the best years of his life, he told me toward the end, his closest approximation of the stability and intimacy of married life. He had known her since his high school days; she was a responsible and thoughtful woman who corresponded with my mother long after my brother had moved on again. How can I fathom what she saw in him? Each morning lighted by that smile, a shining, shallow-rooted blossom glimmering with some decent purpose, some fragile longing for order, with promise and promise and promise again. After my brother died, she wrote to my mother:

> . . . I often wondered if Roger was a lot like his father. From the many things Roger said I often thought perhaps their personalities were similar.
>
> Roger met a man in the Lutheran church as a child and that man apparently influenced Roger's religious convictions causing Roger to believe in a life hereafter and so now perhaps Roger is enjoying a peace that he was unable to find while on earth. I would like to think so. . . .
>
> Hello to all your family. . . . I never met Bill but Roger spoke very highly of him.

Spring 1980. No doubt he did. I learn he has left North Carolina by a surprising telephone call, result of another failed attempt to redeem him-

self: he has enrolled in a community college, has taken a student loan, has dropped out, defaulted, and skipped town. I am listed as closest living relative, the collector informs me. Can you tell me, where is your brother? The voice from out of the telephone is insistent in my ear. "I don't know where he is," I can say truthfully.

I am not my brother's keeper.

X

My brother now is dead, having left three widows and no wives.

He showed up broke and homeless at my mother's again, literally on the wings of a storm, the first tornado in years, driving a wheezing pickup truck through a lurid landscape in which the rain blew sideways and barn roofs walked down the highway. By this time, my mother was living with one of my younger brothers, now a grown man. This brother had his own formulation: "He is an enemy to no one but himself," he said charitably. But the prodigal had returned one too many times; after the first drunken episode brother ordered brother to leave town, and in the wheezing truck he turned south again, to run out of gas and money and drop like flotsam in Jacksonville, Florida. Where he was going is not clear, but one place, it seems, was as good as another to stop, to settle, to resume his life.

None of this is of his own telling, for he never wrote to me. My mother passed on a few selected details if I pried, but she was reluctant always to speak of his disgraces, and I had to seek rumors from others of my family. I heard of him drying out periodically in alcoholic clinics. I heard of an accident at work that had injured his knee. I heard of his new provisional family: a lady bartender who was a great reader, who wanted copies of my books, and her daughter who accepted my brother as her nominal stepfather. And of an actual father who arrived with a gun and rearranged this fragile domestic order. For the last time, my brother came home again.

Home, Robert Frost has written, is where when you go there, they have to take you in. My brother had been reduced to that elemental need: he arrived with a knee brace and a permanent limp, unemployable and fixated on a workman's compensation lawsuit against his last employer. For a while he lived on my mother's couch, then, drawing welfare, he settled into a grimy room a few blocks from downtown, from where he could drag himself to a coffee shop at which he became a fixture, and to a convenience store for his daily load of beer.

Summer 1989. On my occasional visits to my mother, I cannot find him until we meet by chance on my mother's porch; I am leaving and he arrives in a car driven by a friend. For a startled moment he seems to want to flee, then the old smile transforms his face as he limps across the lawn to greet me.

I have not seen him for more years than I can recall. His face is puffy and ravaged; his graying hair is caught back in a short ponytail; his beard is months old and untrimmed. His hands shake with an alcoholic tremor, and his voice shakes as well. It has taken all his courage to turn and meet me.

We talk pointlessly for a few minutes. I have to leave; time is short. "I suppose you know about my condition," he says as I start my car.

I nod. I assume he means his damaged leg. Only later do I learn that cancer has settled in his colon. I send him books in the hospital: Norman Cousins's Head First: The Biology of Hope, *which recounts the effects of humor on the remission of disease. Cousins recommends Charlie Chaplin and the Three Stooges; on reflection, I include Garrison Keillor's* Lake Wobegon Days.

XI

My brother was dying more rapidly now.

He collapsed one day in the coffee shop, clinically dead from heart failure. Only the chance presence of a doctor saved his life; his heart restarted, he was lifted by helicopter to a hospital, where a little balloon, shadowed on a fluorescing screen, forced a passage through his clogged arteries. "The first time ever I was on television," he told me. In time, he returned to his hole of a room and crawled in. His pill and drug bottles mingled with the beer cans and cigarette butts in the litter of his kitchen. He tried to stop smoking but could not. He went to an

Alcoholics Anonymous meeting, only to find it a collection of young men bragging about how many beers they could drink. He was cut up in a knife attack by a drug addict who coveted his painkillers. I have a letter he wrote to my sister, who went to the hospital to collect his abandoned personal effects:

> Sure appreciate you doing this for me. Hope it isn't too much bother.
> I'm sorry we've been out of touch for so long, but you're already gone when I learn you've been here, but of course that has been explained to me. And of course I'm the world's worst at letter writing, ever since I learned that people aren't really interested in what I have to say.
> Not much to say about myself, but for the fact that I'm still hanging in there and looking for something to hope for in my tomorrows. But what?
> My property consists of a garnet ring, a folding belt knife, and a Timex watch. . . .

I tried to see him whenever I was in town. Usually he missed our appointments. He asked me not to come to his room. "I sometimes have company," he said, intimating a woman. But I had seen enough to know that his squalid quarters shamed him, and that his visitors were more likely to be drinking companions.

Summer 1990. Surprisingly, he keeps a promise to meet me for breakfast. He is clean and sober, but his hands shake as he cuts up his eggs, and he wears his long shirt loose around his hips to hide the colostomy bag. He does not smoke, although his fingers are yellow with nicotine. We talk of his lawsuit, still pending in Florida, and of his daughter, who sees him occasionally, and of her half brother, who still considers him something of a father: from such fragments he can conjure up for me an illusory family order. By the end of the meal the strain is showing in his face and voice, and I accept his claim of an appointment with a friend downtown. No, he does not need a ride.

From the booth I watch him limp across the parking lot, hungrily lighting a cigarette as he walks. Out of deep memory my grandmother, dead forty years, rises up to sit silently beside me, and together we who ushered him into life watch him disappear around the corner. Oh, Grandmother, help me now. . . . Her gaze is blank and pitiless, and I know that my brother is already among the living dead.

Summer 1991. I visit him without invitation one night. He sits in his underwear in the heat of the evening, his leg brace on the floor beside him. He is only a little drunk.

"Hand me that towel," he asks, pointing to a dingy rag on the back of the door. He drapes it to cover his colostomy bag. "This is my new asshole. It's only decent to keep it covered."

We talk desultorily over a chasm of fifty years while the black-and-white television flickers silently before us. He speaks to me but keeps his eyes on the screen. In deference to me, he does not light a cigarette. He misses work; he misses the woman in North Carolina. He has thought of writing something about his problems; he has ideas, he has bought a notebook. He is still hopeful of a substantial settlement in his lawsuit; he has ridden the bus to Florida and back to testify. With the money, he can buy a house trailer, grow a little garden, maybe even own a car again. . . . "Oh, hell!" he says suddenly. "I'll probably just piss it all up against the wall."

I am still seeking the easy formulation, for my comfort if not for his. "You sure did inherit all of our father's bad luck," I say finally.

His voice cracks between anger and a sob, but his shoulders straighten with some remnant of self-respect. "Bullshit," he says. "Dad had nothing to do with this. I did it all by myself. It's been a helluva life, but it's all my own."

We embrace awkwardly as I leave. His skin is cool and damp with sweat and he smells like a derelict. The little scar still flares on his chest like the white impress of a finger. He manages another miracle of a smile. "Don't worry about me, brother. I'm going to be all right." Once home, I write him, urging that he set down his thoughts in his notebook. I send him a copy of Norman Maclean's A River Runs through It.

A few months later he collapsed again, clattering down in his room among beer cans and fast-food wrappers; his companion was an alcoholic cousin he had discovered among our numerous relations, a man who had barely the capacity to call an ambulance. This time there is no need for a helicopter ride, no need for a slithering probe along his arteries for the plugged passage to his quiet heart. My brother now is dead for good, and I am not there.

XII

My brother has died a wealthy man. The lawyer has collected half, but my brother had cleared almost thirty thousand dollars in his lawsuit. For a week or two he has been rich and justified, but he has time to spend only a few hundred dollars. There is no sign that he has tried to buy a house trailer, and there is nothing written in a notebook. After his funeral expenses, there will be a good sum for his daughter, a young woman who, against all odds of heredity and upbringing, is leading a decent and orderly life. One more easy formulation: my brother has at last done something right.

October 14, 1991. He has one decent jacket we can bury him in. In his coffin he is barbered, clean-shaven and combed; he has not looked so smart since his portrait at four years old. The mortician's art is to make our dead seem to sleep; charmed, I cannot help waiting for the smile to quicken his face. But his shoulder when I touch it in farewell is like a block of wood.

What cradlesong to ease his way in this last sleep? What blazing sign in the night sky to mark his passage out? What book to send him at his new address? I am startled by the words that form silently on my lips, returning his last reassurance to me. Don't worry about me, brother. I'll be all right.

His burial is like a scene from a sad movie: a small knot of mourners gathered at graveside on a cold and drizzling day. Family only; no friends have appeared from the shambles of his past. After, someone asks me, the family wordsmith, for an epitaph for my brother. I think of his dogged evasion, year by year, of our every ministration to his pain, and I wonder if at bottom such persistence were not a perverse and defining courage. My final lapidary line: "He never missed an opportunity to miss an opportunity."

XIII

My brother now is dead, but the phone still rings for him as bill collectors pursue their prey, and I must answer for him. I dream of him sometimes, a child lurching and falling and rising to fall again as he struggles toward a humming highway; I am paralyzed to reach him. But in my waking reveries, before and after sleep in the quiet hours of the night, another vision rises to freeze me, as in my calm and ordered life I hear the muttering thunder at the margins of the world. On the horizon, lightning strikes and strikes again.

Once, while dusk lingered in the evening sky and snow fell like a benediction on the slumbering earth, time stood at bay as I rocked and sang and held you to my heart, oh my lost brother! But time uncoiling through our decades has broken my voice, and I do not know what words will fill the ragged vacancy in my heart. And now that you are gone, who will stand between me and the gathering storm that nightly haunts my horizon?

Looking for Chandler

Y FATHER SHOOK MY HAND in another good-bye, smiling as usual. "Well, keep your nose clean," he said. "And don't take any wooden nickels."

Over the past few years it had become a formula, a joke each time I went back to school. But this time we stood in front of his car, looking west out over Lake Michigan from where the highway climbed up through the town of Petoskey. Down the road another car waited to take me on my great western adventure. This was in June of 1953, the summer before my senior year at the university. I was two months past my twenty-first birthday; and it is with some trepidation that I revisit now the self I was then and embark with him on our quest for Chandler.

My father and I had spent the night in a cheap motel after the drive upstate from home. Swaggering a little in my fresh majority, I had bought some beer legally and we had spent the evening uncapping bottles and talking about cars. Earlier, I had planned to hitchhike up to meet my ride west, and I was surprised when my father volunteered to drive me this far. He had a weekend off, he said, and he hadn't been north in a long time. We started out in the June dawn, and when I asked he let me begin the driving. His current car was a 1941 Buick club coupé that some previous owner had painted two-tone green with a paint brush and porch enamel. I whipped through the gears as we rolled along the empty streets, and by the time we hit the bottom of Crotch Lake hill, two miles from town, the speedometer needle was bouncing at eighty.

"If you keep it under sixty," my father said, "you won't burn so much oil."

I eased up on the pedal. Traffic increased on the two-lane highway as the morning passed. My hands began to cramp on the wheel, and when we stopped for coffee in Grand Rapids I was glad to let him drive the rest of the way. Except for a leaking radiator hose near Cadillac, we had no trouble; my father tightened a loose hose clamp, refilled the radiator at a farmhouse, and we went on.

I had by this time found my way into the English department at the university. I had dallied a while with the botany department, doing well during our fall field trips among living trees, but my interest had flagged as we came inside in winter and turned our eyes to nature beneath our microscopes; and I foundered completely in taxonomic study, as we unfolded dried specimens pressed in old newspapers, steamed them to pliability over baby-bottle warmers, and dissected them with our *Gray's Manuals* on our knees. I had flirted briefly with the theater program, until I suffered the embarrassment of hearing my voice recorded, an uncertain reed I recognized at once as a gift from my grandmother and sadly inadequate to the inner voice I heard as I read. It was becoming clear that my gifts were with the written word rather than the spoken. I was dazed with my reading of Hemingway and Housman; I was estranged from the girl I loved; and having discovered the world to be a universal tragedy I walked the campus in the autumn evenings, drunk sometimes with beer and sometimes with poetry, in a state of romantic tumescence.

Out of the taxonomic botany class, however, had emerged the western adventure I recount here. I had met Pete Becker in that class and came to know him better as we turned up in the same literature program. He had found a summer job with the U.S. Forest Service; he invited me to join him in his next summer's return. Pete had just been appointed editor of the campus literary magazine, and together we recruited Bob Holloway, a slender, nervous, very bright talker who wrote movie reviews for the *Michigan Daily.* But as the semester drew to its end, both of my new comrades defected. Pete would be married in the summer, and Holloway would remain at home for a job in Detroit. "Can't work out west for peanuts, or pinecones or whatever," he joked, conscious of letting me down. But I found that a girl named Donna was involved in his decision as well. In those days we all seemed to move quite naturally toward early marriages; but I had been bereft of romance, and feeling more than a little abandoned, and with a great adolescent vacancy in my heart, I determined to make the trip alone. What I could not know was that coincidence was preparing another Ann Arbor traveler for the same trip west. I did not know Roger Chandler, but I must acknowledge his entrance into the story here, like the intrusion of King Charles's bloody head into Mr. Dick's mad memorial, for a kind of minor haunting has made this other Roger my companion all these years, and I do not know exactly why.

I had found a ride west with a graduate student in ornithology; he was going to the Olympic Peninsula to study the wing structure of diving birds. And so on this weekend in June my father and I stood facing each other in this most recent of farewells, while my travel companion waited in his new Ford sedan. "Keep your nose clean," my father said. "And don't take any wooden nickels." I left and he left and my journey had begun.

This was some years before the great bridge would span the Straits of Mackinac. We crossed from Mackinaw City to Saint Ignace on the car ferry. As we waited in line to drive aboard I got out and scrabbled in the breakwater for a palm-sized flat rock. Once we were well out on the water I slipped it into a small bundle of letters bound with a rubber band. As the bundle sank into the green waters of the straits, I leaned on the rail and, with a painful self-awareness, felt my heart sink with it. I was twenty-one years old and my life was over.

In the next few days I learned more than I wanted to know about the wing structure of diving birds. My companion would spot and identify roadside birds as we traveled, but his interest was clearly in something wider or deeper, certainly more important. Graduate school was just on the horizon of my consciousness in those days; I had little notion of what it entailed, and this is my earliest recollection of my ambiguity regarding professional study. With some relief I left this companion at my drop-off point in Spokane, where the next day I caught a bus to the ranger station at Priest Lake, Idaho.

This was a staging area where work crews were assembled for the back-country camps; the bunkhouses were filling up with young men—mostly younger than myself, just out of high school. I walked through the rows of double-deckers, looking for my number; on one bunk, already claimed by a duffel bag, I noticed an open copy of *Madame Bovary,* and I made a mental note to look for its owner. My bunkmate was a short, spare young man in jeans, cowboy boots, and a huge white straw Stetson. "I'm Wellborn Judson," he said in an accent I had heard only in the movies. "Just call me Tex."

"Eugene," I said. He looked puzzled. "Your name was probably Eugene at one time. In Latin."

He frowned and removed his hat. "I reckon I'll have to fight you for that," he said calmly. "Do you want to step out back?"

It was a scene straight out of the movies, too; probably he had been defending that name since childhood. This was not the first fight I had ever talked my way out of, but it was the only one that required an etymology lesson. We were on good terms shortly. I promised never to call him Eugene, and he commenced an unending string of tall tales from Texas that became its own lesson in the ascent from fact to fiction to myth.

We were in the panhandle of northern Idaho. The Priest River drains the watershed of the panhandle, flowing from Canada down through the Kaniksu National Forest and the valley of the Priest through Upper and Lower Priest Lake. There were two camps between Upper Priest Lake and the Canadian border; Tex and I were assigned to the further camp, seven miles from Canada itself. A Forest Service bus hauled us on gravel roads another forty miles north to a final staging area at a camp called Hughes Meadows; from here we would move on foot. And here we broke out our newest purchases: calked boots and red crusher hats. The boots were required for the job: I had bought mine at a stop in Missoula for approximately a week's wages. The metal calks ("corks" in the local vernacular) were designed to grip logs and prevent dangerous missteps in the woods. And for added safety we had to "stag" our jeans by cutting off the cuffs so that they would not snag but tear in a fall. The hats, red felt items soft enough to roll up into a duffel bag or to shape to the wearer's taste, were required by local custom. We were issued wooden packboards to strap our gear to; our guide, a tall, lean man about my age with scuffed boots, a faded and sweat-stained crusher, and a full beard, led us across the road to a steep switchback trail that wound up through a densely forested hillside. He moved easily, carrying nothing; behind him labored forty or so new recruits carrying their summer gear on their backs.

There was no road into the Priest River valley. We were climbing the ridge that separated it from the adjacent watershed. To this day that march remains the hardest demand I ever put on my body, not excepting my Army training; and I took some consolation that a few struggled behind me, and some simply turned around and went home. At the top of the ridge we started downhill; I could breathe but my legs were soon like rubber as I braced at each step to keep from tumbling down the descending switchbacks. There was still snow in hollows among the trees.

The trail leveled out again in the river bottoms; it crossed the Priest on a huge pine log that had been felled to make a bridge. Rain was falling in a light drizzle now; we were already wet from the skin out with sweat; soon our clothes were sodden, and some of the red crusher hats were draining pink streams across sweaty faces. The river beneath the bridge was channeled to the width of a two-lane highway; it was swollen and green with snowmelt as it swirled around smooth boulders. Our guide stood on the end of the log bridge and pointed downstream. "If you don't want to try the bridge, there's a ford downstream a ways, where the packer takes his mules across." He strode lightly along the log and headed up the trail without looking back. Top-heavy with packs, one by one we followed him. I later learned that he was under orders to bring us by way of the ford for safety's sake.

The walking was easier now, a level, muddy track through a dripping forest, but I could feel nothing in my shoulders where the pack straps cut in. Two miles further on our guide stopped again, checking names as we straggled up. Below the trail on a flat riverbank was a cluster of tents, the Lower Priest camp. He read off the names of half of us. "You guys will drop off here with me; this is my camp. The rest of you head on up the trail another couple of miles till you run onto the Upper Priest camp."

Without a guide we slogged along. At last I staggered into a clearing full of hanging wood smoke and canvas tents; someone took my name and pointed me to a tent. I found a cot with a sleeping bag. I slipped my pack from my shoulders, and my body seemed to float free from the earth. As feeling flowed back into my shoulders, I unpacked my duffel bag: a few changes of clothing, a jacket, toilet articles, and, at bottom, the measure of my weakness and my strength, my books. "My Gawd!" Tex couldn't believe it. "What you bring all those for? Must be thirty pounds there."

We were all temporary employees of the U.S. Forest Service engaged in blister-rust control. It was simple enough, the camp boss explained to us: blister rust was a fungus that killed white pine trees; it lived half its life cycle, however, on an alternate host, the wild gooseberry, genus *Ribes*. Thus to destroy the ribes would be to control the blister rust and save the pines. Before our camp had opened, a special crew of stringers had marked out one whole slope of the valley watershed. From the top of the ridge to the river's edge they had run kite string in long parallels; at intervals along the string were paper tags marking off units of an acre each. Each of us would be assigned a lane to clear of ribes from ridge to river. We were issued two long yellow hard-braided drag ropes; the idea was to pull one as a marker across our lane, then to return pulling the other a few yards downhill; the space between the two ropes we would inspect for the wild gooseberry, yanking those we found out by the roots. Each morning the foreman would lead us up the mountainside to the top of the ridge and assign us our lanes. This climb was on no permanent switchback trail; it was merely a track straight up, a toe-digging, knee-scraping struggle; and for a while I was among the last to reach the ridge each morning. The foreman eyed me skeptically for a few days, but each morning's climb was easier, and as I hardened into shape, finally climbing with the best of them, I felt like the hero of *Captains Courageous,* my moral stature increasing with my aerobic capacity for hard work.

There was a hierarchy to my new profession. All had started as mere ribes pullers, but those who cleared their lots quickly and thoroughly might be promoted after a few summers to become checkers, who covered several camps spot-checking lots to see if ribes had been missed. A checker might become a foreman, supervising a crew in the field— mainly sneaking up from time to time to see if we were working. Finally a foreman might become a camp boss. We seldom saw our checker, whose work was solitary, although when he did join a couple of us during a lunch break he turned out to be another college student of my age, wearing a plastic military helmet instead of a crusher. As we lounged our half hour away he captured one of the large toads common on the forest floor. He fashioned a cross from two sticks and some string, stuck it in the ground, and tied the toad to it in a rude crucifix. Then he built a small fire of pine needles and twigs around his victim. As the spectacle ended, he grinned, winked, pissed on the fire, and was off down the trail. I have often wondered what finally became his calling.

Our foreman was a furtive, muscular man, also of my age, whose talk was a foul compound of sexual fantasies and drinking exploits: no college man he, but he was vague about his work in winter months. Our camp boss was older by a decade or so, a hairy, sardonic man I discovered to be a doctoral candidate in biology at the University of Missouri. Many summers in the ribes program had taken him to this seasonal eminence. Clearly I had started late in this business, and I was clearing my lots at only a moderate pace.

Our mornings began in gray light as the camp cook walked between the tents banging reveille on a bucket with an ax handle. Our camp boss stood at the entrance to the mess tent, watching to make sure we all washed at the cold-water wash table. "You're not going to pass me food after you've been pulling your pecker all night," he told us the first day. Breakfast was huge: pancakes, bacon, eggs, oatmeal, toast, cookies, fruit, coffee, chocolate. We made up trail lunches from bread and a kind of huge cold sausage that was never called anything but horse-cock. Our work was solitary, dragging our ropes sometimes through brush so thick it was called dog-hair, sometimes across rock outcroppings bare of trees, sometimes through lovely, parklike stands of pines whose lives we were saving. We were allowed a half hour for lunch and two ten-minute breaks, monitored by the foreman, who might be watching us from any concealed vantage. We carried knives to dig large ribes out, canteens of river water, and wads of toilet paper in our shirt pockets. When our canteens were empty we drank from small springs, and when we had to we draped our backsides across fallen logs and shit in the woods like Daniel Boone. We worked through rain and thunderstorms and voracious mosquitoes and some of the most glorious summer days I have ever known. It was grueling, dirty, arduous, sweaty, leg-wrenching, menial, and trivial work, and I could go a whole day without seeing or speaking to anyone. I have never had a job I liked better.

When we came down off the mountain each afternoon, we had hot showers. I still marvel at the ingenuity of the Forest Service plumbing. An earlier crew had built the camp, setting up the tents, digging the latrine and garbage pit, and laying a long coil of fire hose upstream from the camp. Here the hose was attached to a collector box in the river, establishing a head of water pressure sufficient to supply a rude board lavatory, a rudimentary kitchen for the cook, and a wood-fired hot-water heater, all plumbed with a crazy, jerry-built tangle of steel pipes. A log platform with a showerhead above was our great luxury: the cook controlled the hot-water valve, watch in hand, and we each got three minutes to shower. A latrine with a two-hole board behind a canvas screen completed our sanitary arrangements. Laundry we did as best we could on weekends, mostly by tying our clothes to a rope and hanging them in the river current for a day or so. Underwear was a complication and finally an affectation; most of us came to going without. No one shaved. Evenings were filled with talk, mostly lies about women and drinking, and there were card games: these were my high school friends all over again, hardy young men filling a summer between high school and college, and among them I felt ancient by a margin of three years. I was reading Faulkner and James Joyce and *The Golden Bough* and trying to memorize a Robert Frost poem each day.

My tentmates were Tex Judson, a Mormon from Utah named Don, and a very young man whose name I'm not sure I ever knew—he was from Priest River, a local native, and was called simply Nate. He was tall and strong but seemed strangely out of his depth with us, until one night he suddenly confessed that he was only fourteen years old and had lied his age for the job. My Mormon friend was the son of a prosperous rancher, a loudmouth who soon established himself as the camp brownnose, following the camp boss around at every chance. His name quickly became Brownie, I became The Professor, and by the same process a series of inspired names spread through the camp. My favorite was Jim Mackie's: first called Virginia for his home state, he saw his new name transmute to Virgil, Virg, and then simply The Virgin.

At night in the darkness before we fell asleep, Tex astounded us with monumental lies about his cowboy life. He lived, he claimed, with an uncle who was a foreman on the vast King Ranch; he had been bitten by a rattlesnake and had survived by drinking a fifth of whiskey; he had shot a Mexican through the hand to stop a knife fight; he had broken a leg bronc-riding in a rodeo; he had survived a range blizzard by killing a steer, gutting it, and crawling into the warm visceral cavity. My own contributions were lies of a higher order, as I would sometimes recite for them the Frost poems I was memorizing. Unavoidably I was something of an oddity; but I heard rumors of "another really smart guy" from Michigan in the Lower Priest Camp. I identified him with the copy of *Madame Bovary* I had seen, and I idly formed a plan to hike down some Sunday and seek him out. I thought that we might travel home together.

But during my weekend free time I mainly kept to myself. I had found a rocky outcropping from a granite cliff face at the top of the ridge that commanded a view of the entire valley. Below me spread a floor of treetops rolling down to the silver pond that was Upper Priest Lake; beyond my vision, in the sun-filled haze at the horizon, was the lower lake and the town of Priest River. Behind me was wilderness all the way to Canada and beyond. On some days low storms moved up the valley, and at times I was above them. At moments I felt wholly embedded in the natural world, the last man on earth or the first, settled into a vast silence that held no place or need for my voice. I read and watched the sun inch across the southern sky; even Frost was not adequate for what I was trying to feel, and at times I merely watched and dozed against the sun-warmed granite and waited for the chill of night to drive me from my rock.

The daily and weekly rhythms quickly became routine. The earliest interruption was the problem of Tex's blistered heel. New boots meant blistered feet for those not wise enough to wear two pairs of socks. Tex began soaking his foot in hot water from the cook's stove at night, and in the course of a few days a simple blister began to look alarmingly inflamed. Tex added hotter and hotter water and took a few days off work as the pain grew worse. It was the same leg that had been snakebit, he told us, and he went on with a tale of the time his grandfather had cut his ankle on barbed wire: infection had set in, then gangrene. With a skin full of whiskey and a lead bullet between his teeth, he had submitted to the ranch cook, who cut through the flesh with a straight razor, through the bone with a meat saw, and cauterized the stump with a red-hot king bolt. After a few days, Tex's whole foot was inflamed, and the camp boss looked at it with grim worry in his face. "I'm feared I'm gonna lose it," Tex said to anyone who would listen.

Communication with headquarters was by shortwave radio. Word came down to take no chances. Tex would have to be carried out on a stretcher. The camp boss chose the four biggest and strongest among us—I was not one—who would take turns carrying Tex up over the ridge and down to Hughes Meadows, where a truck could take him to a hospital. They left at night with flashlights and Coleman lanterns, Tex tied under a blanket so he would not fall off on the switchback turns. The next evening they returned, smiling broadly, and everyone but the camp boss soon learned that they had brought back a keg of beer from the tavern at Nordman, now hidden in the river, on the same stretcher that had carried Tex out. In another day the radio brought the news of Tex: his foot was simply raw with first-degree burns from hot water. A few days later Tex himself was back, quiet and chastened for a while, until he began to tell us of the nurse who had serviced more than his blistered foot as he lay in his hospital bed.

Bears were a constant diversion. We would meet them in the woods daily as we worked, shy and solitary black bears the size of big dogs, who fled at our approach, and for most of us they held no terror. Aaron Mosko from New York City, however, could not control his fear. Until he came west by Greyhound bus he had never seen unpaved land larger than Central Park, and it was comical to see him back away and look for a tree to climb if we came upon a bear in the trail. Our foreman delighted in sneaking up on Aaron as he worked, grunting like an unseen bear in the brush, to see if he could run him up a tree. And on some nights he would slip melon rinds or meat scraps under the tent wall beneath Aaron's cot, and the bears that roamed through the camp after dark, drawn by the odors of our garbage pit, would snuffle along the tent wall inches from Aaron's head, reaching under his cot to pull out the bits of garbage; one even settled down, head under the tent wall, to munch and snort beneath Aaron's cot itself. One day Aaron started building a bed for himself in the tree where the cook hung the camp meat in a screened box well above bear level. The camp boss put an end to Aaron's torment finally, forbidding the horse-play; but in the woods Aaron was on his own.

As the summer wore on, the bears began to arrive earlier each evening, slipping through the trees like black shadows in the gathering dusk, clustering in conferences of twos and threes on the hillside above the garbage pit. This was simply a hole roofed over with logs, a crude trap-door in the center, and after a while we had to rebuild it almost daily after the bears had pried it open. For a while the cook tried to frighten them away, walking toward them while banging on a pot lid; and then some of the crew began chasing them off, shouting and waving towels. The Virgin began to chase them with a shovel, hoping to land a whack across a hairy rump as they scampered through the trees; soon he began talking about killing one, and he chased with an ax instead of a shovel. I watched as he drew three or four of his buddies into the vortex of his violence, a twilight posse who refined their approaches to a slow stalk until within a few yards of the assembled bears, when with shouts and curses they would charge, swinging axes and shovels, and the bears would scatter untouched to safety in the hillside brush and the gathering darkness. Later, as we lay in our bunks, we could hear them tearing logs off the cover of the garbage pit, and The Virgin swearing.

There came an evening, finally, when one foolish bear doubled back in panicky flight and came down the hillside and through the camp, The Virgin pursuing. At the edge of the river it scrambled up a big pine tree. With flashlights we could just see it, thirty feet up, forelegs

draped over a large limb, eyes glinting in the shifting glare of the flash-
es. The Virgin and his posse gathered below. "We've got him now," he
shouted. "All we got to do is cut the tree down."

The idea took fire in a group larger than the posse. A laughing,
swearing gang of volunteers brought more flashlights and Coleman
lanterns. The camp crosscut saw was pulled out, and willing hands
held lights for the sawyers while others spotlighted the bear. The
Virgin's notion was that the fall would kill the bear, or at least stun it
so that the posse could finish the job. I stood watching with the camp
boss, the foreman, Aaron, and a few others. "What do you think,
Vern?" the foreman asked. "They won't be stopped now," the camp
boss said. "They're bored. They need some excitement. The hell with
it. But I'll bet on the bear."

In the erratic flicker of lanterns and flashlights cursing figures
moved, half in light and half in shadow. The Virgin notched the tree
trunk, and two of his posse began with the saw. It slipped, cutting
someone's wrist; he tied his handkerchief around it and continued.
All fell quiet as the saw began its rhythm, back and forth, inch by inch
through the tree. The bear climbed higher. Something wet splatted
onto the sawyers' heads and shoulders, and they stopped. "He's shit-
ting on us," one of them swore. "Goddamn!" The sawing began again.
We all waited tensely. The tree began to creak and lean. The pair with
the saw pulled a few last strokes, then jumped back.

The flashlights all leaped up to the bear. The tree caught for a
moment in another tree and then eased slowly down, breaking branches as it fell. The bear clambered to the upper side of the trunk and rode
it down, walking the trunk like a tightrope right down to the stump.
For a split second it stood looking at us. The Virgin swung his ax; the
bear ducked; the ax thudded into the tree trunk and the bear was gone.
We could hear it splashing across the river toward the other bank.

In the silence the only sound was the hissing of the Coleman
lanterns. The Virgin began to curse softly. "That's it, boys," the camp
boss said. "Let's get this mess cleaned up." The Virgin was inspecting
the trunk of the fallen tree; he held up something small and black in
the light of the lanterns. "Hey, I got a toe!" he shouted.

I went up the trail to work with Aaron the next morning. Somewhere ahead of us The Virgin climbed with his bear toe on a string

around his neck. The foreman came up behind us. "Hey, Aaron," he said. "You suppose that was the bear you been sleeping with?"

Aaron had been giving the matter some thought. "Listen, Jim," he said. "I been up a tree before. But I ain't never yet shit my pants."

We were a pack camp, not a road camp, which meant that everything came in and went out on our shoulders or on mules' backs. A packer on contract to the Forest Service had brought in all the tents and equipment; he came weekly to bring food supplies and mail. Usually he arrived and left while we were working on the mountainside, but one evening after we had eaten he rode into our camp, on horseback himself with a string of mules behind him. The camp boss treated him with great deference, ordering the cook to rustle up a meal and the rest of us to help unload supplies. I later learned that it was politic to treat this man well; he was obliged only to bring in supplies, the mail was a favor, and if he felt generous he would pack out our personal gear at the end of the season.

The packer was a blocky, red-faced man, bald under his dirty Stetson and wearing the first genuine leather chaps I had ever seen. As we gathered around, he noticed Tex in his cowboy straw hat and high-heeled boots. He tossed Tex his horse's reins. "Here you go, cowboy. Ride Missy down to the river and give her a drink."

Tex stood as though paralyzed. He started to say something, but his voice strangled. He stepped gingerly up to the horse, took the reins awkwardly; with his other hand he stroked the horse's mane. "She's a right pretty filly," he said finally. "I'd be proud to ride her." But he shook his head decisively, his voice gaining confidence. "But I don't think so. I miss my Beauty back home so, and I sort of promised her I wouldn't ride no other horse while I was gone." He turned to our tentmate, the rancher's son. "Brownie, why don't you take her down?"

It flashed on me that Tex had probably never been on a horse in his life. Brownie lifted himself easily into the saddle, turned the horse's head, and took her down the trail to the river. My mind was rapidly completing a life for Tex among the vacancies of his lies and tall tales: I saw him riding his bike along the sidewalks of some Fort Worth housing tract, hanging out in front of some drugstore, dreaming through John Wayne movies, working finally as a shoe salesman while telling his fellow clerks of his exploits with bears in the mountains of Idaho and of the tentmate who recited poetry all night long. As Brownie disappeared toward the river, I looked for Tex. He was headed up the path to the latrine, walking fast.

We stored our week's supplies under the direction of the cook while the packer coiled his ropes and folded the tarpaulins that had covered the loads. He took the mules to water in one long string, then tied them to a picket line between some trees and put nose bags over their sad bony faces. A couple of us gathered to watch and listen to him talk. "Now, these three," he said, motioning to one end of the line, "I just got them this summer and I don't rightly know 'em yet. Call 'em Ike, Mike, and Spike 'cause they look alike."

All dozen or so looked pretty much the same to me, but as I studied them the packer tied off two separately from the string. I could see that these two at least were distinctly different from each other: one lighter colored, lean and rangy; the other dark, plumper and more heavily built. The mule skinner patted one, then the other. "Sugar and Rosebud, they've been with me a long time now. Smarter'n my wife and a damn sight more useful. Better lookin', too. I put Sugar at the head of the string and Rosebud at the ass-end and they just push and pull these new bastards along. I believe I could send 'em up here without me; you-all could unload and send 'em back and I could get drunk at Nordman's Tavern."

He stood with his arms around his two sweethearts, as happy a man as I have ever seen. "Rosebud," I said, my mind skidding into an idiot connection. "Have you seen *Citizen Kane?*"

His glance was puzzled but unconcerned. "You mean that worn out pair of Bob Redman's over at Bonner's Ferry? He had a pair, Abel and Cain, he wanted to sell me."

Probably I had already been in the woods too long. "No," I said. "I was thinking of something else."

Summer drew down into August with little rain and hot, hot weather. The river dropped to a shallow trickle in many places, but deep pools remained backed up behind logjams. There were large forest fires south of us, we heard by way of the camp radio, and many crews had been taken off routine jobs to fight fires. The camp boss remembered something he was supposed to have done in our first week, and one morning we had training in making a firebreak through the woods. But we were not called. The camp boss came to talk with me one evening: at the season's end, he was going to Madison, Wisconsin, to a scientific meeting. It was on my way to Michigan. Would I like to share driving and expenses? I had looked forward to the adventure of hitchhiking all the way home; but the good sense of the opportunity was more than I could deny. Something in Vern's presence made me uneasy, though, and I still hoped to make a connection with the fellow from Michigan in the camp below.

One Sunday early in August, Tex and I hiked down to the camp below ours. Tex, I think, needed a new audience, for some had become openly skeptical of his stories and a few had begun to tease him. With me he felt comfortable; I was perfecting my skills as a listener. I was looking for my fellow Michigander I had heard rumors of. "Oh, yeah . . . Roger Chandler"; they all knew who I meant. But he had gone hiking with a group who hoped to get as far as Lower Priest Lake. "Tall skinny kid," someone told me. "Still has braces on his teeth." Tex and I hung around for a while, then headed back to our camp.

When we came down off the mountain on Monday, the camp boss called a meeting. A message had come over the radio: someone from the lower camp was missing; search parties were being organized. "This kid went off by himself, hiking back from Priest Lake. Wanted to do some exploring. It was already late in the day, and he never made it back to camp." The crew from the lower camp had been pulled off the mountainside to form a search party. We might be called out too. Each day that week a small plane flew up and down the valley, and we came down from work to hear that Chandler was still missing. Tracking bloodhounds had been brought in from Montana, and Chandler's father, a university professor, had flown out from Ann Arbor to join the search. "Ann Arbor," the camp boss said to me. "That's where you're from. Did you know him?" No, I did not; but certainly he had laid his plans in Ann Arbor even as I had laid mine, and certainly he had been with me in that line of staggering men that climbed into the valley of the Priest at the season's beginning. Each day as I scrambled up and down the mountainside, pulling ribes to save the pines, I came to know him. I came to think how we might have met, traveled together, shared a tent, and started on the fateful hike together. I tried to imagine what kind of father a college professor might be. I created a shadow companion out of someone I had never known. Our camp was not called into the search, so I did not get to look for Chandler, but at the end of the week we got the news. Chandler's body had been found in the channel between the lakes. "They think he was trying to come back in the dark and missed the trail. Tried to cross the river on a deadfall, got caught under a logjam. His father was in the boat that found him."

The camps closed early that summer, the Forest Service budget broken by the cost of the search for Chandler. Most of the crew went out at once; but Tex and I stayed on an extra week to break down the camps for the packer to carry out. In one of the tents in the lower camp I found a paperback copy of *Candide.* Chandler's . . . ? Someone must have packed his gear and carried it out. I slipped the book into my pocket. Finally, I saw my duffel bag, books and all, loaded onto Rosebud; then Tex, the camp boss, and I hiked up over the ridge. This time I had no trouble keeping the pace.

A few days later I was in the town of Priest River, officially laid off and ready for my return trip. Tex had ridden off into the sunset on a Greyhound bus, bound for whatever ranch awaited him in the suburbs of Fort Worth. The camp boss and I got a room in the lone hotel; we would leave in his car the next day. We checked in early in the afternoon, and the first thing he did was shave his three months' beard. I considered my face in the mirror: I had noted the other beards growing in my camp, but I had not seen my own face for ten weeks. Though my hair had grown long and waving, the growth on my chin, the color and texture of corn silk, was not especially luxuriant. But it changed the contour of my face, and I liked the way my mustache ran down into the furze below. I decided to keep it for a while, feeling vaguely that I ought to return home with some sign of my life in the woods.

Vern, the camp boss, had been properly distant all summer, but now he became marginally friendly, although the atmosphere seemed always to sour around him. He could speak of friends and family only in derision, and his entry into any topic other than his research began in defensive contempt. He was a strongly built man with an awkward carriage and speech; before he shaved he had reminded me of a movie backwoods moonshiner, and shaving had uncovered an underslung jaw that was better kept concealed. Vern had worked seven summers in the woods since getting out of the Navy; only this summer had he risen to command his own camp. Back in Missouri he was starting a dissertation on the bacterial life of hog wallows. I thought of my ride west with the ornithologist and of my discarded career in natural history: to spend years writing on the wing structure of diving birds or the bacteria of hog wallows struck me as a bizarre displacement of a simple love of nature, and I wondered what comparable displacements might fascinate graduate students in literature.

We had an afternoon and night to kill. The town had several bars; in one of them we found a group of summer workers still hanging on. Vern knew some of the older ones; I made my acquaintance with some of the younger, college students like myself, and I fell quickly into the ritualized round of drinking and storytelling. Silver dollars were still in circulation in the West in those days; I was delighted with them, and I crammed the pockets of my jeans as each round of drinks brought new change. Someone was cursing the dead Chandler: the early layoff had cost some men two weeks' wages. Damn greenhorn. Someone claimed to know that his body was being shipped home by rail from Spokane. Damn greenhorn, riding home in a box, in a boxcar, his father, someone wondered, riding escort in a pullman sleeper . . . We moved from bar to bar, a rowdy crowd the town had tolerated for years, and I walked stiff-legged, pockets jingling with silver coin and belly sloshing with beer. Toward evening we went for a swim at a river sandbar; Vern had disappeared somewhere with some older friends. I rolled my body in the chill and gentle flow of the river current and sank down in the green water to the gravel bottom. I thought of Chandler, I think of him now, rolling in green water beneath a tangle of fallen trees, his cheek against the river stones . . . *(Oh Father! Will you come for me now?)*

As I dried, I fell asleep for a while with my back against a tree; someone woke me in time to get into the bed of a pickup truck to go to a steak house for dinner. My head was pounding and my stomach felt queasy, but steak and onions, hash browns, and more beer anesthetized me into my second drunk of the day. By nightfall we were back in town, settled into a bar with a glowing Wurlitzer jukebox and a greasy buffet of pickled eggs, smoked herring, rye bread, and official Forest Service horse-cock. Vern was sitting at a table with a couple of men and a plump woman older than himself; from time to time he put his arm around her shoulder. Someone tried to introduce me to a drink called a Depth Charge, a shot glass of whiskey sunk in a mug of beer, but I had sense enough to try just one; even in my worst moments, I had generally avoided competitive drinking. Something like a second hunger struck me, though; the pickled eggs and smoked herring gave new savor to the beer that kept arriving, and in a kind of final ritual I washed down one last horse-cock sandwich. I was singing with a new friend to the company of the jukebox:

> Come and sit by my side if you love me,
> Do not hasten to bid me adieu . . .

(Oh, Father! Sing with me now!)

There was a sudden stir at Vern's table; the woman was standing up and shaking her finger at him, cursing. He said something I could not hear, and she turned on her heel and wobbled away. At the door, she paused to shout back at him. "Just for that, you bastard, I'm gonna go out and piss on your tires!" Vern was grinning self-consciously. "Better go after her, Vern," someone shouted.

In ones and twos my friends of the evening were drifting away. Vern and I were sitting at the bar now, nursing beers. Then Vern was down at the end of the bar talking quietly with the bartender; I was concentrating on my stomach, which seemed to be full of silver dollars. Vern made his way toward me, eyes glittering. "They've got a couple of women upstairs," he said. "Ten bucks. Wanna go up?"

I had read enough to know that I was in an archetypal situation. Someone in my voice said, "Sure, why not?" Even as Vern was helping me up the stairs I was trying to recall from all the books I had read what might be ahead of me, something in Hemingway maybe. In my head I began taking notes for a rite of passage.

At the door must have been the only black man in northern Idaho; he took our money, and I had to search for paper because I would not give up my hoard of silver. In a small anteroom lounged two women in sundresses, no longer young, one decidedly skinny, her hair an indeterminate brindle, the other plump and dark. "I get the blonde first," Vern whispered. He took her by the hand. "What's your name, sweetheart?"

Both women had stood up together, blonde and rangy, plump and dark. "My friends just call me Sugar," she said. "Uh-uh, don't handle the merchandise in public." Vern was moving fast now; he and Sugar were already heading down the hall. "You a real blonde?" he asked. The brunette eyed me professionally; she reached out and touched my beard. "You been in the woods a long time," she said. "What's your name, honey?"

I was looking out the window into the alley below, where empty beer kegs lined up like dead soldiers on the loading dock. My mind was in another crazy skid and my stomach seemed to sway around curves. "Chandler," I said. She began a little routine, one worn to a singsong with many tellings. "Say, Chandler, wouldn't it be nice if we could get that mule skinner to pack us up to your camp? Me and Sugar could do all of you guys a lot of good, don't you think? You wanna go to my room?"

I could see the two of them at the picket line in camp, lean and rangy, short and plump, reliable and eager to serve. "She's Sugar," I said. "Then you must be . . . Rosebud!" Somewhere I felt an obscure triumph. "Naw, I'm Irene," she said; "but whatever you want . . . Oh, shit! Chandler, are you gonna be sick?" She pushed open the window and thrust my head outside. Down onto the empty kegs below went my steak and onions, my hash browns, my beer, my Depth Charge, my smoked herring, my pickled eggs, my last serving of horse-cock. The night air was cool and the stars glittered over the pine trees. "Rosebud," I said.

If there had been any passion in the night, I had spent it now in this failed imitation of immorality. I lay down on the floor and closed my eyes. I could hear Irene flipping the pages of a magazine. "You don't get your money back," she said. "I get paid for my time." After a while, Vern came back for Irene. "Think I'll have a little dark meat," he said.

I managed to get up into a chair. Sugar looked me over with some skepticism. "You like blondes?" she tried tentatively. "Did you ever see *Citizen Kane?*" I asked.

We alternated driving and sleeping across Montana, and when we were both tired we rolled up in sleeping bags at the side of the road. Once we had crossed into South Dakota, Vern sought out a backroads detour into the Badlands area; he had an uncle and aunt living near a little town called Interior. He had to ask directions, but we found a small farmhouse and a tumbledown barn and a yard guarded by a flock of fiercely hostile turkeys. I waited in the car while Vern went in. After a while an old woman came out; she wore a faded housedress and an apron above men's work shoes and carried a broom. The air was full of late-summer grasshoppers. In running lunges she batted them down in midflight with her broom, or smashed them as they landed, and the turkeys ran in a vicious, gabbling pack at her heels, snapping up the stunned and wounded grasshoppers.

She saw me in the car. "You some of Vern's family?" she asked, leaning on the broom. I shook my head, and she came near, grinning over a few bad teeth. "I can't stand it when they start talking family," she said. "They're so damn mean, all of 'em." While the turkeys circled the car, I listened and she talked, a litany of complaints against her husband and his family. She had lived on that road all her life, sixty years with her husband. In the winter of 1910 she had lost two children to diphtheria. Burial was impossible until spring; she had lain them beneath the snow in orange crates, marking their places with empty whiskey bottles.

We slept that night in a small prairie cemetery, among tilted limestone markers long untended. I awoke at dawn to a vast rose flush on the horizon; with my back against a gravestone I could feel the earth turning gently into the light, tilting east and returning me home.

At dawn the day after Labor Day I dropped my pack quietly on the front porch of my parents' current home; the front door was open in the September heat, but the screen door was latched inside. My father's car was at home; his truck was not, but that might still be at the terminal.

I dozed for a while in a porch chair until light came full; then I pulled Chandler's copy of *Candide* from my pack and began to read, trying to make sense of his underlinings. Somewhere in Ann Arbor, my shadow companion had come home in a box, escorted by his father.

I heard the pat-pat of small feet on the linoleum inside. My youngest brother, three years old, leaned against the screen door. The hook was above his reach, but the screen had been kicked loose at the bottom of the door, and he squeezed through and stood looking at me. "Hello, Charlie," I said. "Is Dad home?"

He did not know me. I was bearded and long-haired and I wore my red crusher hat. He crept back through the screen and pattered into the front bedroom. "Momma," I heard him say, "Momma, there's a man on the porch."

In the family we laughed over Charlie's mistake, telling and retelling the episode for several days. My father kidded me about my summer beard. "That was no man," he laughed at Charlie, passing me a beer; "that was your big brother." More lately, though, I recall the story more seriously, for I believe that whatever constitutes full manhood, it still lay a little distance ahead of me, over some continental divide I would meander back and forth across without ever marking the line. I do not remember when my father came home, nor what we talked of in the early days of my return, before I went back to school. It was in that week, though, that we went to buy the 1937 Pontiac that he could not have, and when it failed to start a few days later, he showed me how to prime the carburetor with a spray of gasoline from an old Windex bottle. I am sure that when I left for school again, we parted with the old formulaic warning. It meant little to me then, but as I think about it now I realize that I had come home with my nose still fairly clean and my pockets full of silver dollars. In these latter years, it seems to have been good advice, and I am not sure I have had anything wiser to say to my own children.

But certainly as I sat on the porch while morning brightened around me, reading someone else's copy of *Candide* and looking forward vaguely to my last year at the university, I could not foresee my next lurching moves toward manhood, nor the sudden rain of griefs that would test my strength. Within days I would return to Ann Arbor, beardless again, to discover Bob Holloway strolling with his arm around Donna, and it struck me that for the sake of such a lovely girl I too would have foregone a summer in the woods. I found Pete Becker and his new bride installed in a tiny third-floor apartment, leaving me slightly unsettled and jealous at their blending of undergraduate life into domestic bliss. Within weeks, however, I would reclaim the girl I loved, and within months I would stand up to be married for life. Within the year I would be on the road west again, headed for graduate school and a life's career. Hastening to overwhelm me in the near future, a storm of meteor strikes sweeping over my horizon, would be the death of my infant son and the death of my poor doomed laughing improvident father and the suicide of Bob Holloway and early, withering deaths within that charmed cohort of my high school friends. But not every grief loosed in these days would strike in these days; and if one such, early deflected and long adrift, were at last to orbit unforeseen into the tranquil gravity of my middle years, dropping me, like a bullet in the back, undone and unmanned for a dark season, it would have to find its place in another story, one I am not sure I can ever write.

I seem to have fallen into a bit of a strut and fret here, as I come to the summer's end of 1953. What I discover in this spasm so belated, and mourn and celebrate at this distant remove, is, I suspect, simply the end of youth.

Again, though, a simple ending eludes me, for as I have been bringing this summer's chronicle to its natural close, a footnote has been growing, bumping along with increasing weight like some dragging anchor beneath the skiff of my narrative; and as I hoist this weight to the surface a sodden horror emerges and turns a featureless face toward mine. Yes, like poor mad Mr. Dick, I cannot exorcise a long-dead intruder; again and over again, Chandler asserts and inserts himself into my story, and I fear that I too am a little mad. Unable to keep him off my mind, lately I have searched the Idaho newspapers for details of that death in 1953; and Pete Becker, still in Ann Arbor, has copied for me those old pages of local news from Chandler's hometown paper. I try to digest them into my account, but at best I can merely paste them to my own page:

Ann Arbor Youth Found Dead In River

Roger Chandler, 18, Had Been Missing Five Days In Idaho Wilds

(Special to The News)

SAND POINT, IDA.—The body of an 18-year-old Ann Arbor, Mich., youth was found late yesterday floating in the Priest River near here.

The youth, Roger P. Chandler, son of Prof. and Mrs. Joseph P. Chandler of 1516 Montclair Pl., Ann Arbor, had been missing since Sunday, when he left a party of swimmers to explore a forest trail.

A party of searchers, including the youth's father, who had flown to Idaho Thursday to join in the hunt, spotted an object floating in the river. Prof. Chandler identified it as his son.

Details Unknown

Death was officially listed as caused by drowning, but there was no indication as to how the accident happened. Officials theorized that young Chandler may have been walking along the river's edge, slipped, and fallen in.

The youth had been working in a U.S. Department of Agriculture pine blister rust (a disease of pine trees) control camp in the Kaniksu National Forest. The area is in rough, wild country.

A group of the blister rust workers had gone swimming Sunday afternoon. When it came time to return to camp, young Chandler left the group, saying he wanted to explore a trail. He was last seen about 6 p.m. Sunday when he dropped into another disease control camp for a visit.

Bloodhounds Used

As he was an experienced woodsman, there was no immediate fear for his safety. A search was started Tuesday, and a pack of bloodhounds was flown in from Montana Thursday to aid in the hunt.

A June graduate of University High School in Ann Arbor, Chandler was to have enrolled in Michigan State College as a forestry student this fall.

Roger was the Chandlers' only child.

Music Book Fund Established In Honor Of Roger Chandler

University High School classmates of Roger P. Chandler, whose body was found Friday after he had been missing five days in the Idaho wilds, announced today they are setting up a memorial music book fund in his honor.

Funeral services for the youth will be held tomorrow in Priest Falls, Ida., and burial will be there. His mother, Mrs. Joseph P. Chandler, of 1516 Montclair Pl., flew to Idaho yesterday. His father, a University professor of biological chemistry, had gone there earlier last week to join in the search for his son.

The parents asked that no flowers be sent and that contributions be made instead to the music book fund.

Young Chandler had been a celloist and piano accompanist in the orchestra at University High, from which he was graduated in June. His other interests included dramatics and journalism. He was activities editor of the school yearbook and acted as a reporter for The News' Junior, Senior Hi-Notes column.

He had planned to enter Michigan State College in the fall as a forestry student and was in Idaho this summer working for the U.S. Department of Agriculture. He drowned when he apparently fell into the Priest River while exploring forest trails.

Roger was the Chandlers' only child.

A striking young man, no doubt, and just two months launched from home. The carefully nurtured only child of an academic family, something of a paragon himself, I suppose, but perhaps without the need to become one, and without the need to dance for the love of his friends. No mention of an interest in French literature, which leaves me wondering whose book I carried home from his camp, but *Candide* and *Madame Bovary* would have been within his range. I study the high school photograph in the blurred photocopy: a sober, unsmiling young man, lips closed over braces, I surmise. I find no semblance of any face I recall from those days.

I have not puzzled all of this through yet, but certainly I recognize that out of the resentments and vacancies of my own early life I can still envy the privileged childhood of young Chandler—orthodontic braces were rarities in those days, and his University High School offered resources far beyond any I had known, an orchestra even. Something deeper is at work, though, as I try to think of how my own father might have risen, or not risen, to the challenge fate dropped for Chandler's father. I can only believe that it would have been beyond my father's reach and grasp, as were so many of the large challenges of his life; but after all these years I am still willing to imagine my own death as a test of his love. In the interval I have made myself into my image of Chandler's father and, in effect, become a mourning father to myself.

Where my mind stumbles, however, is at the discovery that young Chandler did not come home in a box, did not share my homecoming, but was buried in the Priest River cemetery, forest rangers as pallbearers. I reach for but cannot grasp his father's thinking. What compound of grief and revulsion, what sentiment or principle or convenience, led him to leave behind the poor rag of a thing that had been his son, pulled from the water after five days with the fishes—orthodontic braces, I would guess, the surest sign of who he was?

Clearly, if I would continue this search, the road leads back to Idaho and a headstone in some small cemetery. Good sense tells me that I should drop this little madness now, but I suspect that in time I will make that trip. Meanwhile, under these years of momentum, I continue my search, now for Chandler's father. In *American Men of Science* I track his career and research interests. I find the expected clues in the public record: an emeritus professor at the university, a current address, a telephone number. He would be far advanced in years now, of an age with my father if he had lived. A letter is unanswered, the phone disconnected; but in time I reach a man my age, young Chandler's cousin. Yes, of course: his uncle, Chandler's father, is dead, too, but I have missed him by little more than a year. Finally baffled, I keep thinking that I might have called him, perhaps visited him, presuming on the courtesy of one professor to another a generation younger. I console myself, though, that he has been spared the pain of my inquiry, and I the embarrassment . . . if even I could have framed the matter that had brought me to him. How could I have explained what absurd compulsion had appropriated his son and his grief, or what ventriloquial presence had appropriated my voice, whispering in my throat what I would dare not say: *Oh Father! Now, now I am come home!*

The Girl with the Golden Giggles

WHEN MY YOUNGEST BROTHER called to say that my mother had been taken to the hospital, I was pretty sure the end was near. She was eighty-three, and her heart had been weakening for several years. I visited her twice a year; each time she herself was weaker, and the nitroglycerin pills were always at her elbow. The drive to the hospital was six hundred miles, through and beyond my old hometown, where my mother lived. I arrived late at night and went up to the intensive-care unit in the elevator with a pizza delivery man who was going to the same place. He popped the latched double doors to the unit open with a familiar hand; a buzzer sounded briefly as the doors closed behind us, and two nurses at the nursing station looked up and waved.

My mother was a gasping wrack of bones with a tube down her throat. She opened her eyes when I spoke to her. "Talk to me," she whispered. And so for long minutes I spoke to her of what I had been doing, what my wife had been doing, what my daughters and my grandchildren had been doing. Eventually she closed her eyes and seemed to sleep and I fell silent. It was the longest I had talked to her in all the years I could remember. My hands were shaking. At their station the nurses giggled and talked softly, eating pizza.

My mother outlived my father by thirty-six years. His death had been the last of many crises he delivered to her in their married life; but my brother Roger, seventeen at that time, was already revealing his own knack for disaster, and she would live to bury him as well. And there were the two younger brothers yet to be raised. Truly there would be little peace for her this side of the grave.

No harm was ever intended by my father, of course. He was the best intentioned of men, and there were early years in their lives together that went well and happily enough—at least, until I was born, the first of their children. But then began the series of struggles forward and slidings back that mark my memories of their lives. My father might have made a better life had he married someone strong enough to keep him on a steady track; and my mother might have been a happy, even a charming woman, had she married a man provident enough to shield her from distress. Either case might have yielded fewer children, and made me someone else, half what I am and half what I might have been. But like two innocents they blended their weaknesses in a fatal combination that I can deplore only as I deplore myself.

In her time she told me almost nothing about herself, or about the romance that led to her marriage to my father, and by the time I was grown she had become so distant as to be little more than a ghost in my life. I could approach her with specific questions, but she volunteered nothing and she seemed reluctant and embarrassed to talk about the past. She did leave behind a box of photographs and a few family papers. No one else in the family wanted them, so I took them home to sort over. There ought to be clues among them. There are photographs to be dated, documents to be traced, relatives to query. I am a researcher and a biographer. I should be good at this.

II

There is just one photograph of my mother as a child—a gawky, uncomfortable preadolescent in a sunbonnet, standing with an infant nephew. They might be brother and sister, as truly she might be my aunt's own daughter, such was the difference in their ages. I can get back into the life of this family's baby sister, perhaps, as I recall her in the occasional family gatherings later: talk swirling in two languages as her older sisters and her mother volley in Finnish and English—in one direction for two husbands who speak no Finnish, in the other for my grandparents who speak no English. Everyone has an opinion, a retort, a laughing reply—but two. My mother speaks seldom, hesitant in two languages, diffident even when addressed directly; her characteristic mode is a faint embarrassment. The only one more quiet is my grandfather, who will smile and offer a few words only under direct address. His withdrawal is the silence of the patriarch, hers that of the shy child, although I suspect both sprang from a common ground. So it must have been from the earliest days of her life.

I have given some impression of my mother's father, his dogged, silent heroism, and of my mother's mother, herself a heroic voyager to and in the new world. I can see from later years that the confidence and energy that drove her mother descended in full measure to her older sisters. These women were groundbreakers in the new world. Ina was the eldest, already four when she arrived in this country, bilingual by eight when sister Deeda was born, fourteen at my mother's birth. Ina went to the local Finnish college, became a teacher, married a rising young lawyer, and presided genially over the family the rest of her life: an unflappable, unpretentious woman who wore her intelligence lightly.

I do not know where my grandmother's musical knowledge came from, and I learned nothing of it from my mother—the story comes from my older cousins. Clearly their mothers had talked of the past, and the story reaches to the heart of family life. Soon after arriving in this country, my grandmother drew the outlines of eighty-eight piano keys on a flattened cardboard box, and on this mock keyboard she taught Ina the fingerings of the scales, humming the notes, that she might practice on the school piano. The musical gift descended in larger measure to Deeda, and by her time there was money for a teacher and a cheap upright piano. And ambition had descended in larger measure as well; she practiced incessantly, prodigiously. "She drove the family mad with her constant practicing," Ina's daughter reported, passing family lore to me. "She wore her fingers raw." The effort won her a scholarship to the state teachers' college downstate. There she would meet and marry a handsome athlete and begin a career with him teaching in the public schools.

These futures were already in progress, of course, as my mother grew up, watching and listening. The house would have been full of her sisters' plans and striving, their music and their talk, their mother's encouragement. The models would be in front of her, the paths already blazed, the expectations rampant. Yet somehow she would miss the gifts her sisters had been given. She would show no skill in music, and find neither confidence nor ambition to buoy her up. She was already less her mother's daughter than her father's, I suspect, and the characteristic Finnish gaze, the abstracted vision that withdraws from the moment toward inner horizons, was already an endowment, perhaps latent, from her father. Her mother and her sisters turned vigorously outward into the world. Her father worked the mines in darkness, in wet, seeping pits far beneath the family's feet; at home, he read his Bible and was silent.

She is fourteen. Already she has skipped a grade of school, doing two years' work in one. This is not surprising in her family. She is the last child at home; her parents are in their fifties. Tacitly her care passes from them to her older sisters, already striking paragons, who will lead her into the new world. Ina's life prospers with her young attorney; they have a house in town and a summer cottage. Deeda and her husband are teaching in a small town downstate; her life with a high school coach and teacher has vaulted her into the professional class as well, an arena in which her striving would create a life of careful taste and style. She sends for my mother to join her; certainly there will be advantages. Deeda's carefully made life will become my mother's accident of fate, drawing her willy-nilly into its orbit and fetching her up, in due course, into my father's arms. But first she must finish her high school years.

More documents. I have a transcript of her high school grades. A middling performance overall, so erratic as to suggest talents unfocused or deflected, and full of questions I would like to ask her. Excellent grades in Latin and Spanish, but Cs in French, rising only to a B+ in any English course. Chemistry wobbles from A+ to B-, and a D in public speaking certifies her public diffidence. And yet, teasing evidence elsewhere of amateur theatricals: in the little memory book given to graduating students, I find the first writing in her own hand. One page is reserved for Class Day Events. "Good time," she writes. "Class prophecy. How true will it prove? L. H. Miller and me as vaudeville actors. 'Mustonen & Miller,' 'The Girl with the Golden Giggles.'" She is still only sixteen at graduation; the year is 1926.

(My mother: a vaudeville performer, the girl with the golden giggles. I do not know this person.)

What to do with her life? She might have followed Ina into Suomi College and found a life in the old hometown. But she had been assimilated into Deeda's family for several years; Deeda and her husband had been called to a larger school, and my mother was called to join them. Apparently there was a plan in place, probably with her sisters' vigorous encouragement, for my mother to work for a few years, save some money toward college. Certainly there was all the pressure of expectation that she would raise herself as her sisters had. But for the time being she would enter the world of work and make what she could of it.

The major industry in town was the C. J. Kirsch Company, manufacturer of venetian blinds and drapery hardware. My mother was hired as a clerk in one of the offices. "I remember your mother when she came to town," Mrs. Wagner told me at my father's funeral. "I used to work with her. Such a pretty girl. We were all jealous." Photographs from this time show a vivacious girl, straight dark hair cut close about her face. She has friends her own age, she dresses nicely, she smiles happily, she is something of a clown and cutup before the camera, she is still in her teens. As a benevolent employer, C. J. Kirsch afforded a club room, a bowling alley, and other benefits to make the factory a social center as well; and in February 1928 the Kirsch Club staged an amateur musical, complete with chorus line and costumes. *That's That* was billed as "A fast and furious festival of fun at fashionable Palm Beach." My mother is listed in the program with a small speaking part, and a cast photo shows her in a chorus line of young women "Resorters." Another photo captures a row of young men in blazers and straw hats, the "Stags." At the end of the line is a smiling young man I recognize as my father.

I I I

We had all gathered at the hospital—my sister, my brothers, and I—for my mother's last days. Presently she seemed to rally and was moved out of the intensive-care unit. We all had obligations to jobs and to our families, and we spelled each other at the bedside watch. During intervals I wandered about the old hometown, chasing ghosts. The shabby little house next to the Kirsch Company walls, the home of my seven years' humiliation, had been torn down for a parking lot. The factory whistle no longer blew a daily summons, and the saws no longer whined: everyone now had watches, and metal venetian blinds had replaced the wooden slats of older models. My uncle's house that we had crowded into for a summer was also gone, as were two of the several houses we had lived in out in the countryside and the one-room schoolhouse where I had learned to read. The old county-farm buildings remained, refurbished as a nursing home, and so did part of the little house in the pines, now a kind of rustic lawn ornament to an elegant ranch home set well back behind it.

For the most recent forty years, my mother had lived in the same house. My father had fallen ill there, and after his death he could move her around no longer. In time, one of my younger brothers bought the house, and he and my mother lived for years in a quiet domestic partnership that had eluded her in her years with my father. In one of the coincidences of history, this house was across the street from my father's boyhood home—his mother's home that he had left each morning in 1927 and 1928 to earn his wage at the Kirsch Company factory, to sing and dance in a chorus line, and to court my mother.

He was seventeen and working as a sweeper at the time the cast photos were taken. Probably he had started at sixteen; probably he had pushed his broom through the office where my mother worked soon after she arrived. He was something of a dandy, within his means; off work, he dressed in a suit and tie for outings, affecting a straw boater in summer, later a black Chesterfield overcoat and a black bowler hat, which he called his derby and wore slightly cocked. At age eighteen he gave up his factory job and began as an interstate truck driver. He would pass through town once a week or so, still calling his mother's house his home and courting my mother on the fly. She was still living with her sister as the romance began, and no doubt there were sisterly admonitions, directly from Deeda and by letter from Ina, about this raffish young man drifting irregularly through town. These sisters were not snobs, but they knew the life of a laborer's family in their bones.

Here is a picture of my mother and my father together at this time. On a summer excursion, they face the camera with the easy joy of young lovers. He is eighteen, she a year older. A slender girl with a shy smile and striking eyes, she leans gently into my father's shoulder. He has removed his jacket in the summer heat, but he has kept his vest and his derby hat, slightly cocked. His pose is possessive and confident.

My father was a handsome man in his youth, with a pleasant grin and laughing blue eyes. My grandmother said that of all her sons he was the charmer.

More documents from my mother's box of memorabilia. The romance was at a stage that my mother sent this raffish young man loving birthday cards and valentines, still preserved; but she was apparently also seeing other men. She saved this letter from one of these other charmers:

Dear Ada,

It was impossible for me to come over Monday night although I was in Three Rivers until Thursday. My mother's indisposition has everything upset. It was a keen disappointment for me; more so since I have returned here. I got a wire at Three

Rivers Thursday asking me to come to Chicago to take charge of a large garage. It appears like a real opportunity. I will be in complete charge of the office and mechanics, and if I can make good the salary may be rather large for one of my age. But the disappointment enters here. It will mean very few trips to Three Rivers this summer, if any, so it will be impossible to say when I will see you again. But this is too good to lose. I can arrange my hours to suit my convenience when school begins.

It has been a refreshing experience to have met you. One sees nothing here but painted, brazen, flappers. Necking, drinking and speeding seem to be the order of the day. Small town girls are so much more modest and sincere, and you are a good example of that class.

However, need the fact that I may not see you for some time interfere with your writing me and telling me all about the wonderful country through which we drove Sunday? I suppose you thought me odd, the way I stopped and gazed around, but my keenest joy is getting my feet in real grass and breathing pure air. Give your sister and brother-in-law my sincere regards, and write soon and often. I will answer your letters with pleasure if you will do the same for mine.

Sincerely yours,
J. Arthur Reardon

What a letter! What a young man! A garage mechanic but still taking classes; capable of a literate style, the subjunctive mode, compound-complex sentences complete with semicolons, high moral sentiments, and a love of nature! Here, clearly, is a man with a future. And at the very least a man who might give a young woman second thoughts about an itinerant truck driver with his tavern charm and uncertain prospects. She put his letter away and kept it. She would receive no such letter from my father.

But J. Arthur Reardon was in Chicago and apparently stayed there, preferring to keep his passion, or his sentiments, on paper. W. Cavin Holtz ("just plain Bill," he would say, laughing) would drive hundreds of miles to see her. She seems, though, to have been keeping him at some distance romantically, and although she sent loving cards again the next year on his birthday and on Valentine's Day, she had her eyes fixed on college. I can hear her sisters' anxious exchanges. Surely, Ada will find someone else at college.

I found this newspaper clipping that she had saved: probably it was the first time her name had been in a paper. She is now living independently of her sister, who has gone to another town:

MISS MUSTONE HONORED

Miss Ada Mustone of 202 East West Street, who left today for a summer vacation at her home in Houghton, Mich., was the complimented guest Thursday evening of her co-workers with Mrs. Donald Wetters at the Kirsch Company's plant.

In farewell to Miss Mustone, who will enter Michigan State Normal at Ypsilanti this fall, her friends gathered at Crotch Lake for a picnic supper and made this their last visit together.

I also found photos of my mother and father together that summer, in front of the ivy-covered rooming house at 202 East West Street. She smiles; his arm is around her waist, and his pose is confident and possessive.

IV

The ivy-covered rooming house is also long since torn down, but I remember it. It stood just across the street from my uncle's house, now torn down, where we lived so crowdedly that summer; I passed it often as I walked downtown in my high school years. And I find myself terribly tangled in time in this narrative, walking these streets in my youth and in my parents' youth and in my age, looking for vanished houses in present parking lots as I wait for my mother to die and as I sit here, shuffling through old papers and photographs, waiting for her to decide to marry my father. Watch out for this man, I say. J. Arthur Reardon, where are you?

My mother entered college, following her sister's tracks, in the fall of 1929. The stock market collapsed and the Great Depression began, but I doubt that she noticed. She was proffered a bid to a sorority, she enrolled in a tennis class, she enrolled in English I. These are all the facts that remain, except for a paper she saved from her English class:

THE WORLD OWES ME A LIVING

I am knowledge, conviction. I am that source of information to which the multitude refers with little gusto. I am a body of facts, containing the learning and lore of many ages. I am the wisdom and science of the world. Nevertheless, regardless of all these truths, I am abused, ill-used, blasphemed; considered the least important and most uninteresting thing on this earth. I am the dictionary.

In order to exonerate myself of all these charges, I shall attempt to describe my true value to the world. Different from you humans I am comprised of two interiors. One contains my main organs, all the words of the English language. I am arranged alphabetically, convenient for you to find what you want without upbraiding me needlessly. I include the correct spelling, pronunciation, derivation, definition and usage of each word, with a sentence illustrating its correct meaning. You will find that I like pictures also. Full-page charts, plates and drawings, embracing different subjects are illustrated, some in color. This interior is my chief offering to the universe.

At the beginning I contain a preface, contents, and an interesting story of the words I comprise and directions as to my proper use.

Like most of you people I have an appendix. Mine is divided into different parts. Alphabets of languages, information concerning the sciences, music, tables of weights, et cetera, foreign words and phrases and names of persons and places, comprising geographical and historical appellations.

I hope I have been successful in confirming myself to you. I assure you that when we once become acquainted you and I will be fast friends. I only regret that more do not appreciate me. I am the result of the hard work of many people. Noah Webster was my father. Since then I have been perfected and revised by modern day professors. I have become a work of art, a masterpiece, for your special use and benefit. Hear a dictionary's plea: Do not mistreat me. I am your friend in need. I am only a poor book trying to get along.

Does anyone dispute me now when I say the world owes me a living?

"Strikingly written," the instructor has penned at the top, assigning an A grade. At the bottom a note in my mother's hand (to whom? my father?): "When Ada was a coed!"

Now here is something that, as an English professor, I can work with. What was the assignment? To elaborate an assigned title, or to write in the voice of an inanimate object? In either case, some minor problems in diction and sentence structure, and a loose connection between the thesis/title and the demonstration. But a lively intelligence, a literate style, an ingenious turning of the topic, and a fey sense of humor. Yes, strikingly written. I would look for interesting work from this student.

(My mother the writer. I do not know this woman.)

There was nothing of this charm in the occasional brief letters she wrote to me in my college years. And is it merely a professional impulse that moves me to set this text beside the letter from J. Arthur Reardon, and both beside the only letter I received from my father, which I have yet to quote in its due place? What if my mother had married Reardon—what redoubled genetic code for verbal felicity might have descended to me from that union? Certainly she saved Reardon's letter because it touched reaches in her imagination that my father's occasional scrawls never could, as certainly it has in mine. And who would I be now if not my father's son? O faithless Reardon, upward striving garage mechanic, master of semicolons and the subjunctive mode, do I wish that your blood were a little warmer, your style a little less cool?

My mother did not enroll for the second semester. Instead, she entered a nearby business college for a semester and a summer session, taking a secretarial course. I cannot explain the change. Perhaps money ran short, perhaps she felt the strain of being judged by her sister's performance. Perhaps to shorten the time till she could rejoin my father. I can imagine him parking his long truck near the campus, strolling in his trucker's grease-stained clothing through a crowd of privileged students, searching out her dormitory: a strange venue for him. Weekends she visited her sister Deeda in nearby Highland Park. My father visited her there, on turnarounds from his life on the road. Photographs show them posed affectionately in front of her sister's house, my father confident and possessive.

V

For several days we waited singly and in groupings in my mother's hospital room. The doctor said that her heart was too weak to supply some of her internal organs, which were starting to shut down. Will she be able to go home? Maybe, for a while. His shrug dismissed hope even as he offered it.

She was aware of us and talked briefly, usually to my sister to make her needs known. Sometimes to my younger brothers, but not often to me. They had been her second family, growing to manhood and in daily contact with her after I left home, and they knew her better than I did now. There had been a time she had relied on me to fill my father's place when he was away, but then I had gone off into my own life, and a distancing had begun even before that as I had gathered speed and direction in my march away from the little house next to the Kirsch factory walls. She had handed over to me, unopened, the gift for the disciplined life that had carried her sisters so impossibly far ahead of her, and then she had simply stood out of my way.

I had some work to do in my briefcase, and some reading I wanted to catch up on. While she slept, I opened my recent issue of *The American Scholar* and began to read, making good use of my time.

My parents were married on January 31, 1931, in a justice-of-the-peace ceremony in Goshen, Indiana, just across the state line from my hometown. I believe they went there to avoid a waiting period, for the ceremony was performed the day following the application for license. My mother listed her occupation as stenographer. She was twenty-one, my father twenty, although on the application he lied his age to add a year. They settled in Pontiac, near a turnaround terminal of my father's trucking company, and all seems to have gone well for a while, until I was born in April of the next year. I have the telegram that my Aunt Deeda sent to Ina in upper Michigan: "Seven-and-half pound son born to Ada early this morning. Ada is fine. I was not there but Bill was home. Letter follows."

"Bill was home." It says much about my father's irregular work. It may have meant that luckily he was not miles away on the road, or it may have meant that he had no work at all. The Depression was settling in with harder and harder times by now, and my father's work was unsteady enough that any income was uncertain. My mother and her new baby went home to her parents, far to the north. My father remained in Detroit with what work his trucking company could offer him. The documents reveal a sad and lonely life at both ends, separated for a year. My mother sent the usual valentine again, underscoring the last words of the verse—from one who "thanks her lucky stars that she's *your wife*." Apparently my father did not have regular quarters: the card was addressed to him at the White Star Transit Company of Detroit. In April of the next year I received the only written message ever from the hand of my father, a birthday card with some lines on the back:

> I didnt forget you Son was going to get you something nice for your first Birthday but due to a very sudden increase of business & lack of finances I was unable to do so but that will come later. Better late than never. Give your mother a great big hug and a kiss for me, & Ill be seeing you soon I hope—

No J. Arthur Reardon, this writer. I do not know if he made good on his good intentions, but the lack of finances would be his excuse forever. He and my mother did manage to live together again for the next year. My mother made little moves toward domesticity, buying framed silhouettes for the apartment walls and saving household hints from magazines; and she bought mail-order horoscopes for my father and her new son, but none for herself. She made some of the few friends she could number outside her family. By the summer of 1934, she was pregnant again, and this time she came to live with my father's family.

There was room in the house. My grandmother was recently wid-

owed. Pregnancy was commonplace, even chronic, in that family, and the extended family was large and close by. I was the twenty-first grandchild in a list that would expand annually for years. There were constant comings and goings in a family that embraced my mother wholeheartedly but whose exuberant conviviality could be overwhelming. Her confinement could only have been in a state of continuing embarrassment, among strangers on most days except when my father passed through, hauling new cars that no one in this family could ever afford to buy. After my sister's birth it must have been a relief for my mother to retreat again, now with two children, to her parents' home. She spent another winter apart from my father.

I could go on in disheartening detail. I carry fragments of memory from these days, and I calculate that in their first five years of marriage my parents spent half the time apart. I have continuous memory from age four, when my father gave up the trucking life and we moved from an apartment in Cleveland back to the old hometown, where he went to work again in the Kirsch factory. We lived for a while with my grandmother again, and then in another apartment, and then in small bungalow until my father was laid off, or perhaps on strike. Then a summer in my uncle's crowded house, and then the collapsing little house among the pines, where on that night emblazoned with the aurora borealis my mother brought my brother Roger into the world, and where at age thirty she gave up all her infected teeth to the dentist and became a haggard woman with clicking dentures. And then another drafty rural house, and then a bungalow in town again, and then another farm tenant house where my father worked as a hired man, and then the shabby house next to the factory wall, where my

". . . my father passed through, hauling new cars [here, 1934 LaSalles] that no one in this family could ever afford to buy."

father went back to the trucking life and where my two youngest brothers were born. And then the abandoned county-farm dormitory, and last the little house across from my grandmother, where my father would finally fall ill and leave my mother to spend the rest of her days, longer as a widow than ever as a wife, coping with my brother's self-destruction. Somewhere in this grinding sequence, earlier than I can remember, a light had gone out and the amateur vaudevillian, the camera clown, the vivacious girl with the literate style slipped away, leaving a worn and tired revenant just barely able to cope with each day. I write the litany of a failed and buried life.

As her life eased somewhat in retirement, when she was living with my brother's support, she would sit summer evenings on the porch, or long hours inside, reading with a single lamp. She began keeping scrapbooks of newspaper clippings—train wrecks and massive snows and two-headed calves and archaeological discoveries, as though she were trying to grasp some significance as life floated by. Across the street was the home my father had left each morning, a seventeen-year-old Lothario to court her as he pushed his broom between the office desks. She had been the girl with the golden giggles, who spoke with the voice of a dictionary. I wonder if she wondered where it had all gone wrong.

VI

Time shifts around me like sets on a revolving stage. I have a grand-daughter, voluptuous and vulnerable, of an age with my mother as she first met my father, of an age with my wife when she met me, and I am giddy with revolving time as I think of the folly of teenage lovers in the generations of my family and wait for my mother to die. As I paced the hospital halls I thought to call an old friend from high school, a girl I had dated casually, who lived in town. The next morning I stopped to visit on my way to the hospital. She was attractive still; she had made a good life for herself in a marriage as long as my own, and we talked pleasantly of old friends, our children and grand-children. It was a curious feeling, to be sixteen and sixty inside the same skin.

I wonder what my mother thought as she watched me emerge into my own age of romance. It was a private subject with me, not one I discussed with either parent. I was already pretty much in charge of my own life, and she did not stand in my way. "Nothing was to hold you back," my cousin has told me, repeating family gossip. I suspect that she found me as intimidating in my determined march as her sisters had been in theirs. Life is hard in the family of a paragon. But from her distance she would make little rushes at me, little sudden, embarrassing ambushes that made me more reticent than ever. When I was sixteen, she suddenly handed me an old, tattered sex-education pamphlet and walked away. It was disappointingly saccharine and vague, and I learned nothing I did not already know. Later, I was dating a girl a class ahead of mine; she was about to graduate, and my mother suddenly said to me, as I was going out the door, "I hope you two aren't planning on getting married right away." I was flabbergasted, and I fled. And later still, when I was seriously involved with the girl I would marry, and traveling to see her during college vacations, my mother caught me as I came home one night. "You know," she said, "I could probably have forgotten all about your father if he hadn't kept coming to visit me when I was in college." I have never known if this was a truth or a betrayal.

Certainly a subtle betrayal stalks the lines and pages of this account, as implicit guilt descends upon my poor doomed and laughing father. What chance does he stand against J. Arthur Reardon and the other paragons that measure him in my memory? I see him posed between his brothers-in-law, the attorney and the college athlete, and measured by my aunts' concern for my mother's fate all the years of her marriage, and my heart aches for his humiliation. He felt the distance between the life we led and those of my mother's sisters, and he felt the judgment I had made as I fled our home for long hours in the more comely homes of my friends. "Some folks think they're better than me," he would say, chuckling in derision. "Well, let 'em ride red-eye with me some night, and try and back a freight trailer down a side-scraper alley before breakfast!" He could joke away everything but his uncertain health, mend every broken thing but the life of his family. In between, every greeting and every good-bye was leavened with a jest and a smile, and my mother married him, I am sure, because he made her laugh, he expected nothing of her but her love, and he was not a paragon. J. Arthur Reardon had the mark already on him, and as I reread his letter I hear the voice of a condescending prig.

VII

My next-to-youngest brother, my mother's companion, was the most obviously broken by her decline into this last illness. He it was who kept track of her dentures and eyeglasses and hearing aid and money, and his worry was palpable while the rest of us waited with more composure. He had never married, but had lived with my mother and she with him in a companionship at once comfortable and increasingly narrow. For as long as I can remember, she had often dropped into that deep reverie that I have identified as her father's gift; and when drawn out of it she clearly would have preferred to remain elsewhere. My brother, living with her, slowly withdrew from the world himself, and lives now since her death in an isolation more than a little suspect. At one time he was a popular athlete and class officer, a scholarship student at college; now he works a menial nighttime job, lives without friends and detached from family, watches television and saves his money. So much for the Finnish gaze, in which has foundered another potential paragon.

I have wondered about this endowment that my mother seems to have received from her father and passed on, in different potencies and dilutions, to at least two of us, along with the gift for the disciplined march that came to me unopened from her mother. I have mentioned my own periods of abstraction that sometimes border on the catatonic, and out of which I gather myself to march each day. If I have understood anything about myself it has been in terms of the continuing dialectic between these two poles of my inheritance. But lately, as I try to unpack my early exasperation that my parents should have so bungled their lives, I have begun to detect in this facile schematic a third term in an old betrayal of my father. Much of my own life has been an effort to get right so much that he let go wrong. He gave me nothing, he taught me nothing, finally left me nothing, I long ago told myself. Until in this long-deferred exhumation I find my father's presence, his constant presence, everywhere in myself—in the set of my shoulders and in my walk, in my voice and manner, in my persistence with hammer and saw and every hand tool in the houses I have lived in. I wear my watch on the inside of my wrist because he wore his so, and his wrist turns with mine in doubled gesture a hundred times each day. Mask and model, mold and armor, afford me the skill in each day's march to console myself with the trivial in face of the great and to disarm the world with a jest. It is the next best thing to courage.

The constructed self that served me so well I can understand readily as an adaptation of my father's daily skill. His natural element I knew well: so many times had I sat with him in taverns with the other truckers, or at an uncle's kitchen table with his brothers, as the beer bottles accumulated and the stories exploded in gusts of laughter and he seemed to rise and swell into beery eloquence. Certainly I had borrowed his talents for the daily performance that insinuated me into others' lives. As I have slowed my march I have needed it less, but its vestiges, its feints and dodges, remain a part of my armory for each day's encounter with the world; at times I can feel myself put it on like a jacket, and if I continue with any grace as a social being I have my father to thank. But beneath that extruded self lies my mother's quiet evasion, and beyond that lurks my old silent grandfather, withdrawn God knows where into his Bible and his memories while his family eddies around him. Psychologists would probably murmur about low-grade depression, and they might be right; but my own testimony would add much about the vast simplification and satisfaction in fencing out bores and fools and random irrelevancies as one settles into an internal equilibrium in which little is asked of the outside world. The waters of the inner self close overhead, and as buoyancy lazily diminishes, a cen-tripetal descent begins toward a deepening limit of self-knowledge. I speak now from my own years of exploration of this hermetic realm, as my mother leads me ever deeper, my child's hand in hers; somewhere she passes me on to my grandfather; I sink further and deeper, until my father plunges in to seize my other hand and yank me into the world again. *Where do you go? My wife asks smiling. Where have you been?*

It is an affliction that grips late in youth, I suspect. I am certain it created my mother of the long silences, so different from the laughing young woman in the pictures before her marriage; it has since struck my younger brother with a force clearly pathological. My father's gift for evasive charm would, in its final perfection, destroy my brother Roger as well; and if I have had any luck it has been to survive both afflictions. I can remember the evening, the summer I left high school, when I found with a sudden upwelling of resentment that I could not construct the self I needed to cross the street to join the gang of rau-cous, shoulder-bumping young studs gathered in front of the pool hall. They were my friends, and as I walked home alone through the sum-mer dusk under the great arching elms of our Main Street I found that for too long I had paid in false coin for goods I was not sure I wanted. My center was in their lives, not in my own, and for the moment I pre-ferred my own company and my own inner conversation.

My final insight: it is all very much like reading, like music, like dreaming, like death. This ontological evasion, this slick disappear-ance, this phenomenological shift, this descent into the comfortable pool of the self, has all the seductive charm of the book, the song, the dream, the last sleep. Except that the gaze turns backward into an inte-

Epilogue

*T*HIS ACCOUNT BEGAN ON a late summer day nearly a decade ago as I sat with my family on our screened porch, looking out over our lake. Most of the rest has been written or rewritten here as well, at our summer retreat in the north country. This retreat has been almost the single luxury in a privileged but modest life, possible only by major denials and hundreds of petty economies. Deep atavism works here, of course, reaching back to my own early days on the verge between woods and water. I have lived in many homes, but only here do I never feel that my real life is elsewhere.

I have written almost nothing in this account of the time between my father's death and my mother's—most of my adult life, that is. This period comprises the establishment of my professional career and of my own family—

my love affair with the book and the word, that is, and the deeper love by which I have engaged the primary flow of life as directly and as passionately as I can, and of which, if I would believe Tolstoy, I can say nothing original because it has been happy. But it has also comprised this other establishment, this home between woods and water, as I have been unable to rest easy without another and more permanent grounding, one that I believe runs beneath much of what I have written here.

What has passed for a life's work in the world has still not escaped the doubts I brought back from my summer in the mountains of Idaho, when I heard of the wing structure of diving birds and the microbial life of hog wallows and wondered what comparably arcane goal I might direct my march toward, and what I would do once I got there. I discovered such a goal, and I marched there, and my skill with the book and the word, if not my love of them, has served me on later marches as well. Yet I have not evaded the sense that I have been too often deflected into wing structures and hog wallows when my love was for birds and pigs, that too often my skill has been engaged without my love. At best, my academic life has been a series of flirtations and infatuations without essential commitment. That original trip, however, an attempt to embed myself more deeply in the natural world, turned out to be a journey of discovery—of common corruption, of death by water, of myself: more a meander than a march, and valuable more for the going than for the destination, which turned out merely to be home again. (I resist the impulse to quote several poets here.) So it must have been for the other marches of my life, field trips, more or less timid or daring, around the margins of uncharted wilderness. Even academic exercises in the book and the word afford the pleasure of the skill, and if what I have written here is more daring, it is because it was written for love.

Having meandered into that most potent, most polysemous of terms, I find that I have conflated into it the book and the word, my family, and the wilderness at the heart of nature. I do not propose to disentangle this configuration, except to suggest that there is a wilderness at the heart of all, and that the discipline and daring necessary to compose the first two are nourished in the space I have cleared for them in the third. Certainly I understand that the grand theme of my domestic life has been to recoup the losses of my childhood. How hard

I have worked for that life, before career or other consideration! And how lucky I have been! I have not written of the great romance of my marriage, nor of the family my wife and I have made with great labor and great love, but these have buoyed up everything I have written here; for only out of the confidence of this steady center have I dared to march to the far margins of my early life.

Since this account began, and upon my mother's death, I have received my grandfather's Finnish Bible, redolent of old leather and paper and its language impenetrable to my reading glance, however well I know the text. I have built the sauna I had planned, more elegant than ever my grandfather could have dreamed of, where he can sit with me on the highest bench as I sweat impurities from my spirit. My grandson, no longer an infant, is of a size to stack firewood now; he is by unanimous family testimony growing into a semblance of this grandfather, adept with language and books, disciplined and orderly in his daily life, layered with mannerisms my daughter recognizes, but withal a happier child than the original I remember. Other grand-children have descended regularly in a series perhaps not yet complete; among them the book and the word flourish, and I get fleeting glimpses of other family revenants. There will never be the forty-two my grandmother claimed, but I am content. On weekends and vaca-tions, in different groupings and families, and sometimes all together, the family gathers to eat and drink, to swim and fish, our own small plenitude of aunts and uncles and cousins. There is much talk, and mostly I am silent, mainly swamped by an affection that overwhelms my capacity to respond, although sometimes I sing, a croaking pater-familias, with my grandchildren. Then they are gone, tail-lights wink-ing away into the dusk, my wife and I are alone, and I am content.

So for many days, beneath a canopy of pines and facing a lake that each dawn mirrors the renewal of the world, I read and write and ham-mer and saw in a most seductive solitude. Eagles patrol the sky above our lake, or sit sentinel in the dead trees at its edge, stooping with a deadly hinged grasp to snatch fish from its shallows. They contend with the great breast-beating loons, who patrol the water's surface half submerged, then sink for long minutes to search its depths for prey: sometimes a dropping eagle will strike a prize from the emerging loon's very beak. But by night the lake is the loons' entire, and they call their

mad secrets back and forth until dawn; and when I do not sleep I listen and my heart quickens to another text I recognize but cannot read. By night deer bed in the meadow at our back door. Furtive bears creep out from the dark reaches of the woods; we see them seldom, but they leave their track and their scat in the sand of our road.

In the midst of this mystery I putter at trivial tasks and attempt to redeem my life in words, the one with my father's hands, sometimes with his old tools, and the other with a gift my mother passed unused to me. For years I have sounded the lake with my fishing line, forcing the waters to yield up their secrets; but of late my fervor has slackened as I spend more time with hammer and saw, and I am more often willing to let the loons course the depths for me and report what they find. If time and fortune hold, I shall with my father's help build a new cabin, strong and tight, on the hill above, where in winter we might face this lake and land and the flaring aurora borealis, although in delicate negotiations with my wife she suggests that my cousins who have fled the winter north for California are the wiser Finns. Summers here reveal to me that the fewer people I see, the fewer I have to dance to please, the more contented I become, a curmudgeonly impulse that my working colleagues have seen descend on me through my years among them. No doubt they could spare my company year-round, should I decline into perfected solitude. But I expect a rescue by my father, as has happened more than once.

Meanwhile, my daily dance to please is a private performance, a pas de deux, the ritual labor of love. The woman I have loved so long brings me, as the hour demands, coffee, her love, breakfast, her love, lunch, her love, a beer, her love, her love, her love, her love, in gestures precise and nuanced as ballet . . . to which I reciprocate, measure for measure, in a dance perfected over forty years, and she tolerates my summer beard—graying, grayer, white, as seasons pass—with great good humor. In the evening we watch the sun go down, and night and silence creep over the lake, until the loons begin to call and we take ourselves to bed. Sometimes in the small hours of the night, when I do not sleep and the loons share my watch, a sad and foolish young man I once knew visits me, bearing his voracious heart. We talk for a while, sometimes of Chandler, and he departs, persuaded to be content.

About the Author

WILLIAM HOLTZ is Professor Emeritus of English at the University of Missouri–Columbia. He is the author or editor of several books, including the widely acclaimed *The Ghost in the Little House: A Life of Rose Wilder Lane* and *Dorothy Thompson and Rose Wilder Lane: Forty Years of Friendship, Letters, 1921–1960* (University of Missouri Press).

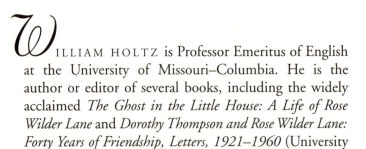